S0-EGH-516

If the doors of perception were
cleansed every thing would appear
to man as it is, Infinite.

—William Blake

MYSTERIES *of* BLACKBERRY VALLEY

Where There's Smoke
The Key Question

MYSTERIES *of* BLACKBERRY VALLEY

The Key
Question

VIRGINIA SMITH AND BETH ADAMS

Guideposts

A Gift from Guideposts

Thank you for your purchase! We want to express our gratitude for your support with a special gift just for you.

Dive into **Spirit Lifters**, a complimentary e-book that will fortify your faith, offering solace during challenging moments. Its 31 carefully selected scripture verses will soothe and uplift your soul.

Please use the QR code or go to **guideposts.org/ spiritlifters** to download.

Mysteries of Blackberry Valley is a trademark of Guideposts.

Published by Guideposts
100 Reserve Road, Suite E200
Danbury, CT 06810
Guideposts.org

Copyright © 2025 by Guideposts. All rights reserved. This book, or parts thereof, may not be reproduced, stored in a retrieval system, or transmitted in any form or by any means, electronic, mechanical, photocopying, recording, or otherwise, without the written permission of the publisher.

This is a work of fiction. Apart from actual historical people and events that may figure into the fiction narrative, all other names, characters, businesses, and events are the creation of the author's imagination and any resemblance to actual persons, living or dead, or events is coincidental. Every attempt has been made to credit the sources of copyrighted material used in this book. If any such acknowledgment has been inadvertently omitted or miscredited, receipt of such information would be appreciated.

Scripture references are from the following sources: *The Holy Bible, King James Version* (KJV). *The Holy Bible, New International Version* (NIV). Copyright © 1973, 1978, 1984, 2011 by Biblica, Inc. Used by permission of Zondervan. All rights reserved worldwide. www.zondervan.com.

Cover and interior design by Müllerhaus
Cover illustration by Bob Kayganich at Illustration Online LLC.
Typeset by Aptara, Inc.

ISBN 978-1-961442-40-5 (hardcover)
ISBN 978-1-961442-41-2 (softcover)
ISBN 978-1-961442-42-9 (epub)

Printed and bound in the United States of America
10 9 8 7 6 5 4 3 2 1

The Key
Question

Chapter One

Bright midday sunlight gleamed through the front windows of the Hot Spot, casting a soft golden glow around the dining room. Hannah Prentiss had spent the past hour sliding the updated menus into protective sleeves. It felt good to get that task done. Scanning the room, she saw a hundred other things that still required attention—the big plate-glass windows could be cleaned, the salt and pepper shakers should be refilled, the silverware needed to be rolled into napkins—but she had to get going.

Hannah put away the menus at the hostess stand before walking through the dining room. She pushed open the double swinging doors that led to the restaurant's kitchen, which was situated in the back of the renovated firehouse. They were still several hours away from seating their first guests today, but on a sunny Saturday in July, Hannah expected a full house, and chef Jacob Forrest was already in the kitchen prepping for dinner.

"I'm headed over to Lacy's to talk about eggs," Hannah called.

Jacob gave her a thumbs-up. "I've got things under control here."

She was grateful to have found a chef with so much experience here in Blackberry Valley, Kentucky. The Hot Spot was Hannah's restaurant, and she worked in the kitchen when needed, but she relied on Jacob's skill as a chef, which had earned them a loyal customer base within weeks of opening.

Walking out into the sunshine, Hannah enjoyed the warmth on her skin as she climbed into her Outback and headed down Main Street. The little town of Blackberry Valley was always pretty, with its quaint streets filled with cute shops and cafes, but the flags waving from lampposts for the recent Fourth of July parade were a nice addition. Beyond the little village, hills rose up all around them, covered in glorious green foliage. Sometimes, Hannah still couldn't believe she lived here. After so many years in Los Angeles, it felt like a dream to have come home again.

Hannah smiled as she drove out of town and onto the rural road that wound past horse farms, with their stately fences surrounding open fields, and rows of corn, lush and green in the summer sun. She passed by the turnoff for a dirt road that led to the entrance of limestone caves under the Bluegrass Hollow Farm cornfields, and then a barn—big and brilliantly red against the deep blue sky—before finally turning into a driveway leading to a pretty white farmhouse with a big front porch and black shutters.

Memories washed over her as she stood in front of the farmhouse she had visited so often as a teenager. How many sleepovers had she enjoyed with her best friend in this house? Her gaze rose to a window on the top floor, centered above the front door and nestled in the center of the steeply pitched roof. She and Lacy Minyard, née Johnston, had spent hours talking on the seat in that window. That was no longer Lacy's bedroom, not since she and her husband, Neil, had accepted ownership of the farm from Lacy's widowed mother and moved to the master bedroom on the main floor.

A pair of horses stood at the wooden fence on the far side of the house, the grass in their pasture even greener than the one where the goats grazed. Their heads hung over the fence's top plank, their gazes fixed on Hannah.

"Hello, Stunner," she called in their direction. "Hello, Misty." She thought that was Razzle Dazzle over on the far side of the pasture.

As if they'd been waiting for her acknowledgment, they both tossed their heads before withdrawing from the fence.

"Hi, Hannah!" Lacy stepped out onto the porch in khaki cargo shorts, boots, and a T-shirt, her reddish-brown hair in a messy ponytail. "Good to see you."

"You too."

Lacy trotted down the steps and across the driveway to the mailbox on the side of the road. A hand-painted sign that said FARM-FRESH EGGS hung from the bottom of the mailbox. She opened the little metal door and pulled out a stack of envelopes.

She led Hannah inside the house, which was blessedly cool. The shade from the trees around the house made it a respite on the hottest summer day. Lacy led her past the parlor, through the living room where a half-done jigsaw puzzle waited on a side table, and into the kitchen.

Lacy gestured at the table. "Have a seat," she said. "Lemonade?" She set the stack of mail on the table next to a notebook, pen, and her phone.

"Please." Hannah sat down in a cane-bottom chair. The kitchen still had the same wooden cabinets that had hung here when they were kids, but Lacy had painted them a grayish blue and replaced the old laminate counter with butcher block.

Lacy set two glasses of cold lemonade on the table as she sat. "Let's talk eggs. I'm thrilled that your restaurant is doing so well you need more. Right now you're getting fifteen dozen a week. How many more do you need?"

Bluegrass Hollow Farm had been passed down through Lacy's family on her father's side for generations. When Lacy's father, Frank, had passed away, her mother, Christine, had transferred the farm to her daughter. Lacy had grown the farm's chicken business to a very profitable level, which had worked out well for Hannah. She was passionate about sourcing quality ingredients from local farms for the dishes at the Hot Spot, and Lacy had been supplying eggs since the restaurant opened.

Hannah took a sip of lemonade. It was exactly the right combination of sweet and tart, and she was pretty sure Lacy had made it from scratch, judging by the flavor and the bowl of fresh lemons sitting on the counter. Hannah cocked her head as she considered the question. "Since I'm open five days a week, and only for dinner—"

"Which I still think is a mistake," Lacy interjected. "Blackberry Valley has no good place for brunch on Sundays. If you provided a local option, most people would stay in town rather than drive the thirty miles to Bowling Green."

"I would, but then I'd have to work every Sunday." Hannah shook her head. "I'd never be able to go to church, and that's important to me."

"There's that." Her friend tapped the pen on her notebook. "So, how many more eggs?"

Taking another sip of her lemonade, Hannah thought through the list of current offerings. The Hot Spot's menu would change with the seasons, since she planned on using locally grown produce whenever she could. Kentucky's vegetable offerings in early July were plentiful and diverse, which meant the new menu brimmed with variety.

"I use them in desserts, of course. And in the breading for the chicken tenders." She used her fingers to tick off items. "Some of the salads have them. And I use egg yolks in my cheese sauce."

"No kidding?" Lacy cast a grin her way. "No wonder your Hot Browns are so rich and yummy. I figured you had a secret ingredient." The Hot Brown was a Kentucky classic, an open-faced sandwich piled with roasted turkey, bacon, and tomatoes on thick slices of hearty bread and pulled together with a cheesy topping.

"You figured right. And I'm thinking about changing up our Hot Browns, for what it's worth."

"Why? They're so good!"

"Maybe I can make them even better." Hannah had been thinking of trying out a new spin on the local favorite. It would be a bit risky, since the dish was a longtime statewide tradition, and Hannah was well aware that messing with tradition could be a problem around here. But if she was right—and she usually was about food— her special twist would be a hit with the locals.

But that was beside the point now. She continued to think through the menu. She didn't need eggs for most of the dinner items—the Five Alarm Burger, the Flamethrowers Chicken Wings, the Pull Box Sandwich, and the Rookie Meltdown Sandwich were all big sellers so far, but none required eggs. Jacob liked to make specialty baked goods when he had the time, but standard items like the buns came from a local bakery, Sweet Caroline's. But there was a new item on the menu.

"If last night was any indication, the Breakfast Burger will be a high-demand item. So I'll need eggs for that."

"I had a bite of Neil's last night," Lacy said. "That fried egg on top is inspired."

"Glad you liked it."

"Of course, the bacon didn't hurt either."

"Does bacon ever hurt?"

"Good point."

Hannah did a quick mental calculation. "Can I get twenty dozen a week?"

The question held a good amount of hesitation. Though Lacy had assured Hannah that her chickens were more productive than ever, and her egg business was booming, that many eggs every week seemed like a big ask.

"Done." Lacy jotted a note in her notebook and then closed the cover with a snap. "That's no problem."

"Really? You have that many?"

"My ladies are very happy, so they produce a lot."

They talked about pricing, and even with the increased amount, the number seemed more than fair.

"More lemonade?" Lacy asked.

Hannah shook her glass gently, and the ice tinkled softly. "I wouldn't say no."

Lacy refilled both their glasses then started sorting through the stack of mail. "Why do all the bills arrive at once?"

"It almost always happens that way, doesn't it?" The second glass of lemonade was just as good.

Lacy flipped through the envelopes, stopping when she came to a padded manila envelope. She squinted at it. "That's odd. It's from my mother."

"Why would she mail something to you?"

"I don't know. If she has something for me, she usually gives it to me. I mean, she has an apartment in town." Flipping over the envelope, Lacy opened it and slid out a thick packet of white tissue paper. Inside was a piece of yellowed fabric, folded to form a pouch. Nestled between the folds of cloth lay a metal object.

"It's a key." Lacy picked it up and held it between them. "A heavy one."

"That's interesting." It appeared to be quite old and made of brass. The shaft was round and thick, with notched teeth on a plate attached near the end. The head was an ornate oval, carved with some kind of design. It was about the same length as Lacy's cell phone.

Lacy held it in her palm and hefted it a few times. "I wonder what it unlocks."

"Your mom didn't include a note?"

"I don't think so." Lacy set the key down and dug back through the packing material. "No note, but she wrapped it in this weird handkerchief."

Spreading the fabric on the table's surface, Lacy pressed out the wrinkles with both hands. Around nine inches square, the edges had been trimmed with lace. An elaborately—but crudely—embroidered *M* faced one corner.

"It's not weird. It's pretty."

"But I've never seen it before. And what's the *M* for?" Christine's last name was Johnston.

"What's your mom's maiden name?"

"Knicely, with a silent *K* at the front."

"I bet she had to spell that one a lot for people."

"Mom always jokes that she married Dad for his last name. You almost never have to tell people how to spell Johnston." Lacy stared at the handkerchief for a minute then shrugged. "She probably pulled it out of the rag bag to wrap this in."

Hannah picked up the key to inspect it more closely. It was indeed heavy, likely solid brass. Definitely old, or at least fashioned to look old, with a burnished glow. She squinted to see details in the decorative scrollwork on the key's head. "It's a mountain," she said. "Is your mom into mountains?"

"I don't know how to answer that question. Everyone likes mountains."

"Everyone doesn't like mountains."

"Name me one person you've ever met who is anti-mountain."

"Well, okay, no one is *anti*-mountain." Hannah chuckled. "I had a friend in California who didn't like beaches because of the sand. He didn't like how it got everywhere and everything in your home is gritty for days after you go to the beach."

"Why in the world did your friend live in Los Angeles if he didn't like the beach?"

"I don't know. My point is that some people might feel the same way about mountains for whatever reason."

"I think my mom is fine with mountains," Lacy said with a straight face.

"Does she like to hike? Or ski? Or have some particular fondness for mountains?"

"I don't think she's ever tried skiing, and I've never known her to willingly go on a hike."

Hannah tapped the scrollwork. "So why would she send you a key with a mountain on it? And for that matter, why did she mail this to you instead of coming by the farm?"

"Or giving it to me at church tomorrow." Lacy set down the handkerchief and picked up her cell phone. "I'm going to see what this is about." She put the call on speaker as it rang.

"Hi, honey." Christine's familiar voice came through the phone. "I was about to call you."

"I'm here with Hannah, Mom. You're on speaker, FYI."

"Hello, Hannah," Christine said. "How's your dad?"

"He's doing fine, Mrs. Johnston. Thank you for asking. He was at my restaurant on Thursday."

"Hannah, I've asked you not to call me that."

"Sorry, Christine. It feels disrespectful, I guess."

Christine laughed. "We are practically family. I can assure you I prefer it when you call me by my first name."

"I'll try," Hannah promised.

"Anyway, Mom, I got your package, and I'm kind of confused."

"Hold on." A note of surprise entered Christine's voice. "What do you mean you got my package?"

"The one you sent with the key and the handkerchief inside."

"The key and handkerchief *I* sent? You sent those things to me, along with a note I can't read because much of the ink is washed away."

"What?" Lacy's face betrayed the same confusion Hannah felt. "I didn't send you a package. I got one from you."

"But the envelope says this package came from you. Though I'm guessing your confusion means you aren't the one who sent it, any more than I sent the one you got," Christine said.

"I did not," Lacy confirmed. "So who *did* send them? And what are they about?"

Christine was quiet for a moment, and then she finally said, "I have no idea. But I guess we'd better figure it out."

Chapter Two

Fifteen minutes later, Christine arrived at the farm and walked in through the side door that led directly to the kitchen. As happy as Hannah was to see Lacy's mother, it also brought a fresh wave of grief. She wished she could call her mother and have her come over. Mom's death eight years before had left a hole in her heart, an empty place that still ached at odd times.

"Let me see your key," Christine said, dropping a padded envelope of her own on the table. She picked up the key Lacy had gotten in the mail. "This is very similar to the one I received."

Lacy opened the padded envelope addressed to Christine and slid out the handkerchief, key, and paper. She picked up the key. "You're right."

Christine held both keys in front of her face and tilted her head back to peer at them through the bottom half of her bifocals. She laid them side-by-side in the palm of her hand. "You know, with them right next to each other like this, I do see some differences."

Hannah and Lacy both leaned close.

"They must fit two different locks," Hannah said, "but they're probably connected. They have the same design."

"I have no idea what they unlock, though," Christine admitted. She had the same reddish-brown hair and hazel eyes as her daughter, though her hair was streaked with silver, and she had laugh lines around her eyes. Seeing them standing there with their heads together, it was like Hannah was looking at a picture of Lacy now and thirty years from now. "Do you?"

"No idea. Hannah thought it might have something to do with mountains."

"Well, that's a logical conclusion, I guess," Christine said. "But I don't know anything about which mountain it might be."

"So you're not anti-mountain? Hannah thought you might be." Lacy grinned.

"What are you talking about? No one is anti-mountain, Lacy." Christine peered at them. "Honestly, you girls are silly sometimes."

Despite the strangeness of the situation, Hannah felt a sudden urge to laugh. She'd seen that exact expression on Christine's face—confusion, exasperation, and barely hidden amusement—so many times growing up, and it was fun to see that they could still spark it.

"What's that paper?" Hannah asked, trying to get back on track. She gestured to the folded page smeared with blue ink that Christine had taken out of her envelope.

"I'm not sure, honestly," Christine said. "It looks like some kind of poem or something. Or it used to be." Christine picked up the paper and unfolded it. "It got wet, though, so the ink has run."

Hannah examined the page for herself. It looked like a poem had been copied out in peacock-blue ink, but at least half of the words were obscured.

"'Long years,'" Lacy read. "Something 'cannot fill—'"

"'The absence,'" Christine read. "Some smeared words, and then, '—and years.'"

"This line ends with 'they were fire,'" Hannah said, narrowing her eyes. "That's an odd phrase."

"And this last line ends with 'and understand.'" Lacy straightened up. "That's a whole lot of nothing. What are we supposed to make of that?"

"It would no doubt make sense if we could read the whole thing," Christine said.

"I imagine it's meant as a message of some kind," Hannah said.

"Well, it might as well be in another language for as much good as it does me," Christine said.

"How did it get wet?" Lacy asked. "Did someone put it in there like that?"

"Now that would be a cruel trick," Christine said. "Let's hope no one is truly that diabolical."

Hannah picked up the padded envelope and turned it over in her hands. There was a small tear in one corner, cutting through both the yellow paper layer and the plastic bubble wrap layer underneath. "It appears the envelope was damaged in transit somehow." The whole corner of the envelope was a slightly darker yellow, and there was a wavy line that marked where the water had spread to.

"Well, that's unfortunate," Lacy said. "It's too bad we can't see the rest of it."

"It is too bad," Hannah agreed. "Can I see your handkerchief?" Maybe she could make more sense of that.

Christine slid the handkerchief across the table and Hannah picked it up. She unfolded it and saw that it had the same elegant *M* embroidered in dark blue thread. This one too looked like it had been done by an inexperienced hand, featuring various lengths of stitches, crooked positioning, and an untidy underside.

"You don't know who *M* is?" Hannah asked.

"Not a clue," Christine said.

"Is there any chance it's a *W*?" Lacy asked, rotating it.

"Don't letters usually face the corner?" Hannah asked. "It's facing the wrong way if it's a *W*."

"I don't see a lot of handkerchiefs these days, but that makes sense to me," Lacy replied.

"It looks old." Christine ran her fingers over the stitching.

"It would have to be," Lacy said. "Like I said, who even uses handkerchiefs anymore, let alone monogrammed ones?"

"It does hearken back to a different time, doesn't it?" Christine said. "It seems so civilized, honestly."

"Seems unsanitary to me," Lacy said with a grimace.

"In any case, I haven't seen anyone using one in my lifetime," Hannah said. She continued to study the handkerchief, running her fingers gently over the soft fabric and the lace trim. "Lacy."

Lacy turned to her. "Yes?"

Hannah indicated the lace trim. "I mean, the handkerchief is lacy. Do you think…" But she let her voice trail off. She wasn't even sure what she was getting at.

"I didn't send it, I promise you," Lacy said.

"I know that. But I was wondering whether it might be a signal of some kind." The words sounded ridiculous to Hannah even as she said them.

"Like it was meant for me?" Lacy held up the envelope. "The fact that it was addressed to me told me that already."

"I don't know." She was grasping at straws. But there had to be something here. Something to tell them who had sent these packages, and why they'd decided to make it look like Lacy and Christine had sent them to each other. "What about the handwriting? Do you recognize that?"

Both women studied the writing on the envelopes. The names and addresses had been printed with black marker in the same handwriting.

"It's different than the writing on the poem," Christine said, comparing the smeared piece of paper to her envelope. The writing was indeed different, the envelope letters all uppercase and composed with a confident hand, while the poem appeared to have been written in script by a shakier hand.

"Well, I'm stumped," Christine said. "I don't understand."

"I don't either," Lacy said. "Maybe there was supposed to be an explanation somewhere, and it got lost. Maybe it fell out through the hole in the envelope."

"Maybe," Christine said dubiously.

Hannah thought it sounded unlikely too—the hole was tiny—but didn't want to say so. "If we can't figure it out, it can't be all that important, right?"

"I suppose." Now Lacy sounded unconvinced.

They were all quiet. For a moment, the only sound was the ticking of the grandfather clock in the hallway. Then Christine said, "You repainted the pantry door."

"Yes," Lacy said, sounding as startled by the observation as Hannah felt. "I've been meaning to do it for ages, but we're slowly getting around to things, one at a time."

"You didn't like the yellow?"

"It's not that we didn't like it. It just didn't go with the colors in here anymore," Lacy said carefully.

Suddenly the air had grown tense. Hannah didn't understand why, but she decided to stay out of it.

Christine eyed the door for a moment, and then she finally nodded and said, "It looks nice. You've done a great job updating this place."

"Thanks, Mom." Lacy smiled, but her eyes remained guarded.

"Well, I should probably get going," Christine said. "I'm supposed to pick up Melba in a few minutes. She convinced me to try a water aerobics class, Lord help me." Hannah recognized the name of Christine's best friend. Because she worked as a nurse at the elementary school, Christine was off for the summer, and Lacy had said she was taking advantage of the time to try new things. "But I don't know what to do with all of this." Christine indicated the key, the handkerchief, and the poem. "It's not the kind of thing the police would investigate, is it?"

"I doubt it," Lacy said. "Not unless they turn out to be stolen or something like that. But we don't have any proof that a crime was committed."

"More likely it's some kind of joke," Christine said. "Though I don't have any clue what the point of that would be, or who would think it's funny."

"There must be a way to figure out who sent them," Hannah said. She wanted to understand what was happening here. This was too great a puzzle to simply ignore. "Would it be all right if I took a picture of them? Maybe I can figure out what's going on."

"That's fine with me," Christine said, and Lacy agreed.

Hannah dug out her phone and snapped photos of the keys, both handkerchiefs, and the smeared paper that had been in Christine's envelope. She also took pictures of the envelopes themselves, front and back.

"Thank you, Hannah." Christine gathered her package and its contents then headed for the side door. "Let us know if you figure it out."

"Tell Melba I said hi," Lacy called. Christine waved in acknowledgment and left. Lacy sighed when the door closed behind her.

"What's up?" Hannah asked at once.

"Nothing. I'm sure she doesn't mean anything by it."

The mysterious tension became clear to Hannah. "The pantry door?"

Lacy nodded. "I know she spent decades cooking in this kitchen, so she still sees it as hers. She can't help it. But it almost seems like a personal affront to her every time we change something. It's a struggle to make this place feel like our own when she still feels like it's hers."

"It sounded like she was trying to be okay with it, at least," Hannah said.

"She is, but I can still tell that it bothers her. It took her a month to come to terms with it when I put new curtains on the window over the sink."

Hannah tried to choose her words carefully. "I'm sure it's hard to see changes in something that holds so many memories for her."

"I know. And it's all wrapped up with her recollections of Dad, so it's wonderful and painful all at once. I mean, they were married for almost forty years, and this house has echoes of him in every corner."

"Was it weird, having her move out so you could move in?" Hannah had still been in California when that happened, so she had missed most of it.

"It was weird. In fact, I didn't want her to go. We begged her to stay. We said she could use the first-floor suite, or take over the whole upstairs, or whatever she wanted. She said we'd want our space, so we offered to fix up the cottage on the east side of the property— the one she and Dad lived in when they were first married, before Grandpa passed and they took over the main house. But she didn't want to. She said it's our home now and she wanted a fresh start anyway. I must admit, I was a little annoyed. Why did she want to move out so badly? But she was insistent."

"It would be nice to have her so close."

"I thought so too. And I worry about her without Dad. But she wanted to move out, so we respect that. But that makes it annoying when she comes back and gets upset about the fact that we're making it our own. Like, wasn't that what she told us to do?"

"I'm sure she doesn't mean it that way," Hannah said. "I'm sure she wants you to be happy here."

"Yeah, probably." Lacy leaned against a countertop. "You know what would be another advantage of having her live here?"

"What?"

"This whole key thing wouldn't have happened. There wouldn't be any question of mailing things to each other," Lacy said with a smile.

Hannah laughed as she checked the time. "That's very true. And on that note, I'd better get going. If I don't get back soon, Jacob will revamp the menu, even though we recently updated it. He was trying to talk me into a rack of lamb yesterday."

"That does sound good, but it might be a bit too fancy for the locals." Lacy grinned. "Thank you, Hannah. Did you mean it when you said you'd try to figure out who sent these things?"

"Of course I meant it."

"Thanks. I can't help but think—well, I keep wondering if it could be something important. And I don't have the slightest clue what it's about, but I want to find out."

"Don't worry," Hannah assured her friend. "We'll figure it out together."

Chapter Three

When Hannah stepped into the restaurant, she was met by the aromas of chicken roasting and meat loaf baking. Her stomach grumbled. She realized she hadn't eaten lunch.

"Whatever that is, I want it," she said, and Elaine Wilby, the hostess, laughed.

Elaine was wrapping silverware in napkins while Dylan Bowman, the restaurant's young waiter, refilled saltshakers. From where Hannah stood, it looked like he was getting as much salt on the floor as in the shakers.

"I'm sure Jacob will let you have a taste," Dylan said.

"I wouldn't count on it," Elaine replied.

"I'll test my luck." She pushed through the swinging doors to the kitchen. "It smells good in here."

"This tenderloin looks particularly good tonight," Jacob said, using a sharp knife to carefully slice off thin rounds.

"It's organic, so it's a bit more expensive, but we'll see what the customers think." Hannah picked up a fresh biscuit from the cooling rack and broke it open. She pulled a butter knife from a drawer and a jar of Dijon mustard from the fridge, and spread the mustard on one side of the biscuit. "I hope they like it, because it comes from a farm nearby I'd love to support."

"I bet they'll like it," Jacob said. He batted her hand away from the freshly sliced pork. "If you leave them any, that is. This is for our customers."

"Fair labor laws stipulate that the staff must be fed," Hannah replied, snagging a slice anyway.

Jacob rolled his eyes then jerked a thumb over his shoulder. "By the way, the fridge is on the fritz."

"What? It's brand new." Aside from the renovation of the old firehouse, the walk-in fridge was one of the biggest investments she had made in opening the Hot Spot. "What's wrong with it?"

"It keeps shutting off for short periods. I noticed it a couple times this afternoon. I'd go in there and everything was fine, and then a while later, it would be off, but then it would come back on."

"It didn't get too warm, did it?"

"No, we're fine as far as health codes go. But I thought you might want to have someone come out and take a look at it."

"I'll call my dad." Her father, Gabriel Prentiss, was a retired electrician. Hopefully he could tell her whether the problem was with the electricity or with the machine. "This is fantastic, by the way."

Jacob gave a small smile. "I can't say I disagree."

Hannah laughed at his implied admission that he'd tried the pork as well.

She called her father, who promised to come over to check it out, and then finished her sandwich and focused on preparing for another busy night. By the time the doors opened at four, the dining room was bright and clean, and the smells coming from the kitchen made her mouth water.

The first guests to arrive were a charming couple who reminded Hannah of her grandparents, who lived not far away in Park City, about twenty minutes from Blackberry Valley.

"It's my wife's birthday," the man said.

"I'm seventy-six, and I don't feel a day older than when I married this old geezer fifty-two years ago." She gave her husband a loving smile, and he beamed back at her.

"Fifty-two happy years with the best and most beautiful woman around." He pressed a kiss to her temple.

"Well, I'm honored that this is how you wanted to spend your birthday," Hannah said. A part of her wondered if she'd ever find a love like this couple clearly had, one that would last until they were old and gray and still joking around together.

She turned to Elaine, who was smiling right along with everyone else. "Please show these two to the best table in the house."

"Of course. Right this way." Elaine took two menus and guided them to a two-top by the window. When she returned to the hostess stand, she told Hannah, "They're so sweet."

"They are indeed," Hannah agreed.

"Being married for that long is something to celebrate, even if they are here for a birthday," Elaine said.

Hannah wasn't sure how to respond. She knew that Elaine was a widow with a college-age son, though she didn't know how long she'd been married.

She was saved from having to reply when a new customer came into the restaurant. Hannah guessed the customer was in her twenties, with blond hair, big brown eyes, and dramatic eye shadow. "Oh my goodness, this place is so cute," the young woman said, taking in the high ceilings, brick walls, and firehouse paraphernalia that dotted the walls. "Did it used to be a fire station?"

"It did," Elaine said. "This is the owner, Hannah."

"I'm Madison. It's nice to meet you. Oh my goodness, I love it." The girl clapped her hands. "This whole town is such a dream. I've visited so many cute boutiques, and that coffee shop is adorable, and everywhere I asked, they said that this place has the best food in town."

"I don't know about that," Hannah said at the same time Elaine said, "You heard right."

"Well, in that case, I'd love a table."

"For one?"

"Just me," Madison confirmed.

"Right this way." Elaine grabbed a menu and led her to a table in the corner.

While Elaine was busy, Hannah greeted a group of women enjoying a girls' night out. Then Dad came in, toolbox in hand. She ushered him to the kitchen, where he set to work examining the refrigerator.

Hannah spent the next half hour making sure things were running smoothly, expediting orders in the kitchen, jumping in to refill waters, and sneaking in an advance order of the raspberry and peach pie for the birthday couple's dessert. The girls'-night crew seemed happy, Madison smiled as she dipped her fries in ketchup, and the dining room had the hum of excited conversation.

Dad emerged from the kitchen. "Solved your problem."

"What was it?" Hannah asked eagerly.

"A, uh, loose connection with the wall," Dad said, grinning. "I pushed the plug fully into the outlet, and now it's fine."

"You mean I called an electrician to tell me to plug the fridge in?" Hannah felt a bit silly. True, Jacob was the one who had brought the issue to her attention, but he'd probably noticed it in the middle of several other things. He wouldn't have had a chance to investigate, but Hannah should have.

"Luckily, this electrician doesn't charge his favorite customer. You were only being cautious. I'm happy to report both the fridge and the wiring are fine."

"I suppose that is a good thing."

"I'm glad you called, because I've been wanting to talk to you about something anyway. Can you spare a minute for your old man?"

"Of course."

His gaze slid to Elaine, and then returned to hers. "Walk me to my truck."

Her curiosity piqued, Hannah followed him through the front door.

Dad opened the door to his pickup and placed his toolbox on the floor in front of the passenger seat. "I was over at the church the other day cleaning muck out of the gutters, and your name came up. Do you recall Mitch Thomas? Young guy, about your age. Dark hair. Clean-cut. Sits on the right near the back on Sundays."

"I think so."

"You like him?" His tone was casual. Too casual. An alarm began ringing dimly in her ears.

"I don't like or dislike him," she said with extreme care. "I haven't exchanged more than five words with him." She narrowed her eyes. "Why do you ask?"

He gave a careless shrug. "Just wondering. He's not married, you know."

The alarm's volume kicked up a notch. "You don't say."

"Divorced, but it wasn't his fault. They married young, right out of high school, and things didn't work out. No kids."

Hannah faced him, folding her arms over her chest. "What are you getting at, Dad?"

"I'm not getting at anything," he replied with a shrug. "Except he's a nice guy, and he was asking if you're seeing anyone, and I figured—"

"Dad." She held up a hand. "I'm not interested in going out with him or anyone else. I feel like we've talked about that before."

He studied her for a long moment, his lips twitching with unspoken words. Then he inhaled a long breath through his nose. "Okay. Just thought I'd mention the fact that he was asking about you."

"Thank you for telling me." She rose on her tiptoes to plant a quick kiss on his cheek. "I just started a business, and that's taking all of my attention. Until the Hot Spot is firmly established and financially successful, I don't have time for anything else. Okay?"

"Understood." He slid behind the steering wheel.

Hannah stepped back as he closed the door. "Thanks again for coming so quickly and reminding me to plug in the fridge better," she told him through the open window.

His answer was a tender smile. "Anything for my favorite girl."

The truck's engine roared to life. She stepped up onto the sidewalk and waved as the vehicle rolled down the street, their conversation replaying in her mind. Her father trying to fix her up with a date? She shook her head. There was something particularly weird about that. Being close to family was the primary reason she'd left California and returned to Blackberry Valley, but there were some things that would take some getting used to.

Back in Los Angeles she'd dated here and there, but never allowed anything serious to develop. Working as a chef in a high-end restaurant was a demanding job to which she'd devoted all her energy. There simply hadn't been time for romance then, and she had even less time for it now. Maybe someday, when her life settled a bit, she'd find time to develop a relationship.

An image rose unbidden to her mind. Liam Berthold, Blackberry Valley's fire chief, had been super helpful since she'd returned to town. He'd generously loaned her a generation's worth of his family's antique firehouse memorabilia when she decorated the Hot Spot, even though he'd been investigating a house fire at the time.

Hannah shoved the image from her mind. Liam was a friend. There was no reason for her to think of him at the moment. She shook her head and walked back to the restaurant.

Checking in on the kitchen, she saw that they were getting a bit behind, so she jumped in to plate burgers and cook fries. Though she always enjoyed being in the kitchen, it was mindless work, and her thoughts drifted back to the snippets of poem she'd read earlier that day.

Long years... cannot fill—
The absence... —and years

"What's that?" Jacob asked.

"Oh, nothing," Hannah answered. She hadn't realized she'd spoken aloud. "I'm talking to myself."

"As long as you don't start arguing with yourself and losing." Jacob craned his neck toward the shelf where several plates waited. "I don't know where Dylan is. Do you mind taking these to table twelve before they get cold?"

"Sure thing."

Hannah would worry about that poem later. For now, she had a restaurant to run.

Chapter Four

The lawn of Grace Community Church blazed bright green in the sunlight. Hannah inhaled the heady scent of freshly cut grass and fragrant lavender. The purple blossoms had exploded across the field beside the church building. She made a mental note to contact the farm owner and arrange a purchase. Lavender lemon cookies and lavender-infused lemonade would make wonderful seasonal additions to the Hot Spot's menu. And she wanted to try her hand at a recipe for lavender and sumac roast chicken.

A familiar voice drew her from her musings. "And how's my *little* sister?"

She turned to look up into the smiling face of her younger brother Drew, who delighted in standing close so that she had to crane her neck to see his face. When they were kids, she had relentlessly poked fun at him for being short, but he'd enjoyed a late growth spurt after she left for college in California.

"Busy," she responded airily.

"Hi, Aunt Hannah," shouted Andrew's oldest child, nine-year-old AJ, as he dashed past them.

"Hello," she called after him as he disappeared into the church building.

"Hi, Hannah," said Allison, Drew's auburn-haired wife. She held tightly to the hand of five-year-old Axel, who was attempting to pull away and follow his older brother.

"Dad said you called him to plug in a refrigerator," Drew said, smiling.

"Word travels fast."

"That is *not* what your dad told us," Allison said, elbowing Drew. "Your dad's point was your restaurant was busy and he was glad to see you doing so well."

"Also, that you had to call an electrician to plug in a fridge." Drew grinned.

Hannah beamed at her niece, who stood between Drew and Allison. "Goodness, Ava, you look pretty today. Is that a new dress?"

Dimples appeared in the girl's plump cheeks, and she twisted back and forth, the hem of her dress swishing around her legs. "Mama bought it for me for the Fourth of July." Then she became serious. "I didn't get to light the sparkler because I'm only seven. But AJ did." She cast a glare at the church doors where her older brother had gone.

"But next year you'll be eight," Hannah reminded her. "Maybe you can light one then."

Ava turned a hopeful expression up to her father.

"We'll see." He directed his attention to someone behind Hannah. "There's Liam. I need to talk to him." He strolled off with a long-legged pace.

"They're talking about setting up a regular bowling night," Allision told Hannah. "I told him he's welcome to do that, as long as we girls get equal time."

"That sounds good to me." She recalled the group of women who'd been in the restaurant doing some similar female bonding. They'd looked like they were having fun.

"We'll have to get one on the calendar. In the meantime, you're off tomorrow, right? Do you want to come over for dinner?"

"Grandpa Gabe is coming over," Ava announced. "And so is—"

"Zeus," Allison interrupted her daughter. "Gabriel is bringing Zeus, like he always does."

Dad certainly loved that dog and brought him most everywhere. "Sure. That sounds nice." The restaurant was closed on Mondays, so Hannah was free in the evening. "I'm looking forward to it."

Hannah tried to concentrate on the service and Pastor Bob Dawson's sermon. She really did.

But it was hard, when both Lacy and her mom sat in the pew in front of her, and all she could think about was those envelopes that had arrived yesterday. Scanning the church, she saw so many people whose names started with *M*—Lacy and Neil Minyard, for one thing.

Neil's parents, Heath and Bronwen Minyard, sat on the far side of the church. Could they have had something to do with it?

Then there was Hannah's cousin Maeve, her uncle Gordon's daughter. Maeve sat with her husband, Hunter, and their three kids. Hannah couldn't see how Maeve could be involved. Maeve and Lacy were friendly, but they'd never been especially close, and she didn't think Maeve knew Christine particularly well.

There was Marshall Fredericks, the food critic at the local paper. But that didn't even make sense. She was making things up at this point, casting suspicion on anyone whose first or last name started with an *M*.

Perhaps she would do better to focus on the keys. What could they possibly unlock? It was most likely a building of some kind. And with that decorative carving, it was probably some kind of antique building. Something like the courthouse. Or the Blackberry Inn, housed in a historic home across the park from the restaurant. But why would someone send keys to Lacy and Christine to open any of those places?

And why the mountain symbol on the keys? There weren't any mountains around here, but there were plenty of hills. Did that mean the key unlocked something on one of them? She tried to imagine what was even in those hills that could be locked. It wasn't very populated up there, and the farther one got from town, the more isolated the surroundings became.

Her cousin Ryder—Maeve's brother—liked to go camping and backpacking up that way. Maybe he would know of an old cabin or something of that sort. Or maybe an old mining tunnel that had been locked up for decades, with strange sounds coming out of it at night, and—

From the front of the church, Pastor Bob Dawson announced the number of the final hymn, and Hannah realized she'd missed most of the sermon. As they sang "Great Is Thy Faithfulness," Hannah made a plan for what she would do when the service ended.

When the last note of the song ended, people began gathering their things, and Hannah slipped out of her pew. She made it to

Maeve's row while she was collecting the crayons and coloring pages that littered their pew.

"Hi, Maeve."

"Good morning, Hannah." Maeve smiled, still shoving crayons into boxes. "How's it going? Just a minute, Paxton," she said to her six-year-old son, who was trying to squeeze past her to get to the fellowship hall, where coffee hour treats awaited.

"Good. It's—um—" Now that she was here, Hannah realized she should have thought this part out. "I was wondering, did you lose a handkerchief recently?" It was a pretty lame opening, she had to admit.

"A handkerchief?" Maeve's brow wrinkled. "No, I don't have any handkerchiefs."

"I didn't think so. I mean, who uses handkerchiefs these days, right?"

"Exactly. Why do you ask?"

"I came across one with an *M* embroidered on it recently, and I'm trying to find the owner," Hannah said.

"Well, it's not me." Maeve said. "Paxton, do not crawl under the pews."

"I'll let you go," Hannah said. "I saw that coffee hour involves cinnamon rolls today, so I can see why this guy is eager to get there."

"I'll see you around," Maeve said.

Hannah walked down the aisle to the back of the church, thinking that Maeve probably thought she was a little crazy. She scanned the sanctuary, but Ryder had disappeared in the time she'd been chatting. Maybe she'd be able to catch him outside.

She hurried out, blinked rapidly in the bright sunshine, and glanced around for Ryder. She spotted him in the shade of a dogwood tree, chatting with Liam Berthold.

"Hey, Hannah."

She turned to find Lacy and Neil approaching.

"Hello." Hannah hugged Lacy and gave Neil a little wave. "I saw you inside, but didn't get a chance to speak to you."

"You were a woman on a mission," Lacy said.

Hannah grimaced. "Not a useful one, sadly."

"Maeve didn't know anything?"

"Not a thing."

"Well, we've only been on the case for a day," Lacy said. "Are you doing anything this afternoon?"

"Not really, aside from some cleaning and a hot date with a mystery I picked up at this great little shop." She grinned at Neil, who owned Legend & Key Bookstore, where he sold new and used books of all kinds.

"Thank you for your patronage," Neil replied.

"Care to come over for lunch? I had an idea about the keys," Lacy said. "I thought we could test it out."

"That sounds great. Can I bring anything?"

"No, we'll have a sandwich and chips or something."

"*Eggceptional* egg salad, I presume?" she joked.

Lacy snorted. "Okay, we're heading out, but we'll see you soon."

Movement out of the corner of her eye caught Hannah's attention. Mitch Thomas strode in her direction, a smile on his face.

Her conversation with her father about Mitch sprang into her mind. She had meant it when she said she wasn't interested in dating. She didn't want to be rude, but she also wanted to catch her cousin before he left. An artful conversation during which she tried to let someone down easy would risk her missing Ryder.

She flashed a quick, apologetic smile at Mitch then went to meet Ryder and Liam under the tree. "Hi, you two."

"Hi, Hannah." Ryder was a couple years younger than Hannah, and he was taller and very fit. She knew many women in town thought he was attractive, with his close-cropped dark hair and defined jaw, but to Hannah he would always be her annoying little cousin. "Good to see you. Liam and I were talking about a cave we want to explore over by Cave City."

"Oh. Cool." Hannah tried to act casual, as if that was why she had come over to join their conversation. "I love caves."

Ryder laughed. "Now I know something strange is going on. I tried to take you into the cave on the Johnston property when we were kids, and you started to hyperventilate. There are lots of things you love, but caves are definitely not one of them."

"Okay, fine. They're dark and full of spiders, and I get claustrophobic. What matters is that I have a question for you."

Ryder squinted behind Hannah and must have spied Mitch. "Ah. Now I understand the sudden desire to talk to us. Boy problems, Cousin?"

Hannah felt her cheeks redden. "No. I wanted to talk to you, though now I'm second-guessing that."

"An urgent question, apparently, judging by how quickly you got over here as soon as Mitch stepped outside."

"Go easy on poor Mitch," Liam said, smiling. He wore a button-down that emphasized the warmth in his brown eyes. "He's a nice guy."

"I don't know what you're talking about," Hannah said, lifting her chin. "*Anyway*, I wanted to ask you about what's up in those hills." She gestured around vaguely at the hills that surrounded the town.

"What do you mean?" Ryder cocked his head.

"Are there any old buildings that would have locks on them out there? Like, abandoned cabins or anything like that?"

"Why?" Ryder asked. "Are you searching for something to fuel your nightmares?"

"No, I am trying to figure out what these might open." She took out her phone and pulled up the picture of the keys she'd taken yesterday.

"Oh wow," Ryder said. "Those are some fancy keys."

"They look extremely old," Liam said.

Hannah quickly explained the situation then zoomed in on the mountains etched into the ends of the keys. "This is what made me think maybe they open something up in those hills. You've been all over them, so I thought if anyone knew what's up there, you might."

"Well, there is an old abandoned cabin I found one time when I was hiking along the Lincoln trail," Ryder said. "But it was way up there. I don't know who used to live there, but the place is very isolated. And you wouldn't need a key to get into what's left of it. You could probably knock it down with a stiff wind."

"There's the entrance to the old Carruthers Cave," Liam said. "They sealed that off years ago, after—"

"I know. Those teenagers, back in the eighties," Hannah said solemnly. It wasn't the only cave in town where someone had gone in and not made it out. "That's why I can't understand why anyone would want to go poking around inside them."

"Who knows? Anyway, there's a big, industrial padlock on the gate they put up over the Carruthers Cave entrance. I'm confident that this old key wouldn't fit into that lock."

"Yeah. I can't think of anything up there that would require a key of this sort," Ryder said. "Sorry."

"If we think of anything, we'll let you know," Liam added. He glanced in Mitch's direction and then returned his attention to her. "Why don't I walk you to your car?"

"I would be most grateful," Hannah said.

"I hear you make a killer peach pie. Would you be that grateful?"

She chuckled. "I do. But I don't know that an escort to the parking lot is worth all that. Do you know how annoying it is to peel peaches?"

"Suit yourself," Liam said, and started to turn away. From here, she could see Mitch's face brighten.

"Peach pie it is," Hannah blurted.

Ryder smirked. "What a hero."

"A good cousin would have escorted me for free," Hannah told him.

"Unfortunately, I'm not a good cousin," Ryder answered.

Liam took her arm. "Let's connect this week about next weekend," he said to Ryder.

"Sounds good. And let me know when you get that pie, and I'll come help you eat it."

"It's cute that you think I'll share." Liam started walking in the direction of Hannah's car. Hannah couldn't help but notice how strong his arm was and how nice he smelled, like sandalwood and soap. "I feel kind of bad. Mitch is a nice guy."

"He is," Hannah said. "I just don't want him to get the wrong idea. I'm not interested in dating anyone right now. I'm trying to get a restaurant off the ground. We've done well so far, but longevity is always a concern in the restaurant business."

"I see." Was she imagining it, or did his tone change? "It does take a lot of work to get something like that going."

"It's pretty all-consuming," she said. Though, truly, at this moment, the main thing consuming her thoughts was how nice it felt to have his arm wrapped around hers. She steered him to her car under a redbud tree.

"In that case, I'm happy to be your escape route whenever you need me," Liam said. "As long as there's pie involved. Though, honestly, it would be kinder to tell poor Mitch the truth."

"I know, but my mind is elsewhere today, and I don't have the attention span to give that conversation the kindness he deserves." They were at her car now, and she dug her key fob out of her bag and unlocked the vehicle. "I'll bake that pie this week. How about I text you when it's ready?"

"Sounds good. You have my number?"

"I do."

"I'd better check. Here, hand me your phone."

They'd texted plenty of times while she'd been trying to figure out the source of a mysterious fire a few weeks back. He knew she had his number. But she handed him her phone anyway and waited as he typed something in.

"Now you've got the right contact info," he said as he handed it back. "Good luck with those keys."

"Thank you." She opened the car door, and a wave of hot air rushed out. "I'll be in touch about that pie."

He gave her a cheerful thumbs-up and headed for his own car.

Hannah sat, started the engine, and waited for the air streaming from the vents to cool down. She went to set her phone on the console and noticed that Liam had changed his name in her contact list to *Liam "The Hero" Berthold*.

He was ridiculous. But as she drove off, she couldn't keep the smile off her face.

Chapter Five

Hannah parked behind Lacy's pickup truck and stepped out of her Outback. The horses were in the pasture, but the baby goats bounded around in their pen, climbing on the wooden crate Lacy had put in their enclosure.

She caught sight of Lacy on her way to the chicken coop and went to join her friend. A handful of chickens scattered before Hannah, clucking a symphony that she interpreted as irritation at being forced to move out of the way. A trio fell in beside her and strutted along at her side. Though she couldn't be sure, she thought she recognized the rust-colored one.

"Hello, Hennifer," she said to the hen, who didn't acknowledge the greeting. The bird's red wattles swayed as she walked on her toes, her head jutting with every step.

Up ahead, Lacy halted at the gate enclosing the chicken coop and waved at Hannah. "You're just in time to give me a hand."

"With what?"

Laughing, Lacy shook her head. "I've got some pullets that are ready to be introduced to the flock."

"What in the world is a pullet?"

"You'll see." Lacy led her toward the back of the chicken run, where a second, smaller area had been fenced off within the larger run. Inside were a dozen or so birds, identifiably younger by their smaller size and underdeveloped tail feathers.

"Aw, they're so cute," Hannah said. "Why are they isolated from the others?" She bent down to stick a finger through the wire mesh. The young chickens skittered away from her.

"For their own safety," Lacy told her. "There's a very strict pecking order in any flock. If new birds are added too quickly, the dominant ones will pick on them. These pullets have been here for over a month, since they were fluffy yellow chicks. The others have gotten used to them by now."

Lacy unlatched the gate and stepped through. Sensing a new threat, the birds raced to the back corner of the pen, clucking in alarm.

"They're not used to me yet, though." Lacy addressed the chickens. "It's time to move on to bigger and better things, my fowl little friends."

Hannah laughed aloud as she watched the chickens scurry around the small enclosure in their attempt to escape Lacy. Their clucking took on a hysterical note as they dashed every which way, including into one another.

"Sometimes they need a bit of encouragement," Lacy said, her words holding a barely concealed chuckle.

Hannah entered the pen to help, which caused a fresh wave of frenzied cackling. Together they shooed the chickens out of their small pen.

Finally, Lacy latched the gate behind the last stragglers. "Now go make friends," she told the chickens. "But you might want to stay away from Rocky for a day or two."

She looked up, and Hannah followed her gaze to the top of the coop where a huge rooster perched on the peak. Rocky's head cocked sideways as he fixed beady black eyes on the newcomers below.

"Rocky doesn't like teen chickens?" Hannah asked.

"He can be a bit territorial." Lacy planted her hands on her hips and called up to the rooster. "You be nice to the new arrivals, you hear? If you pick on them, I'll lock you in the holding pen."

Rocky gave a disdainful ruffle of his impressive feathers.

Chuckling, Lacy motioned to Hannah. "Come on. I've got lunch on the table, as long as Neil hasn't eaten it all."

The two exited the chicken run and headed to the farmhouse's back door. They had nearly reached the porch when a car pulled from the main road onto the narrow gravel driveway.

"Are you expecting someone else?" Hannah asked.

Lacy shaded her eyes with a hand. "No, and I don't recognize the car."

The blue sedan rolled to a stop behind Hannah's Outback, and a woman about their age climbed out of the driver's seat. Two young kids peered out from the back seat. "Hi. I saw the sign at the road. You sell fresh eggs?"

"That's right. I sell them by the dozen or the tray, which is thirty. How many would you like?"

"Just a dozen, please."

"I'll be right back." Lacy disappeared inside the barn, where she kept an old refrigerator stocked with cartons.

"They are exceptionally good eggs," Hannah told the woman. "I recently increased my restaurant's regular order with Lacy."

"You have a restaurant?" the woman asked.

"I do. I own the Hot Spot."

"Oh, that's the one in the old firehouse, right? I passed that on the way in. I'll have to try it sometime."

"Please do," Hannah said as Lacy came back out from the barn. "We'd love to have you."

"Here you go," Lacy sang out as she returned. "Have you bought farm-fresh eggs before?"

"I have not." The woman took the carton. "I'm looking forward to trying them."

"There are a couple of things to keep in mind," Lacy explained. "They might appear dirty, but don't wash them."

"Oh?" The woman opened the carton and inspected the contents. "Why not?"

"Because God created eggs with a natural protective layer that keeps them fresh," Lacy explained. "If you wash that layer off, your eggs won't last as long."

Her eyes widened. "I had no idea."

"Also, you don't need to refrigerate them," Lacy added. "They'll last for weeks on the kitchen counter. Just wash them before you crack them. If you dip them in warm water and then let them sit for a few minutes, the dirt will wipe right off."

"Interesting." She closed the carton. "How will I know if I've kept them too long?"

"There's a trick to that. Fill a bowl with room-temperature water and drop an egg in. If it sinks to the bottom and settles on its side, it's fresh. When an egg begins to get a little older it will start to turn on its end and bob up to the surface. It's still fine to eat, but it loses a bit of flavor. You might want to hard boil that one, or maybe use it in a recipe."

Hannah listened, fascinated. "What does it do if it's no longer good to eat?"

"It floats," Lacy said. "If an egg floats, don't crack it open in the house. Get rid of it outside."

"You are a wealth of knowledge," the woman said. "How much do I owe you?"

Lacy named her price and then took a white plastic card reader from her pocket. "I can take cash or credit."

"Credit, please." The woman retrieved her phone. "I never have cash."

"I don't either." Lacy held out her phone for the woman to tap her credit card against.

Lacy's phone dinged when the transaction went through. "Thank you!" Lacy called. The woman waved and climbed into her car. Lacy and Hannah waved back and stood watching as the car backed into the grass to turn around. The tires crunched on the driveway as she neared the exit. Neither spoke until the vehicle turned onto the main road and headed for town.

They started toward the farmhouse. The barn, where Lacy's father had kept dairy cows, looked beautiful against the cerulean-blue sky. Which reminded Hannah of something. "Hey, do you know any local organic beef farmers?"

Lacy answered without hesitation. "Amos Bowers." She gave brief directions to the farm.

Hannah remembered Mr. Bowers from when she'd grown up in Blackberry Valley. "I thought of him," she said, "but I didn't think he would still be in business."

"He's still strong as an ox and working his family farm. He did hire a couple of workers a few years back, and I was glad to see that he was delegating some of his workload," Lacy said. "I'll give you his number."

They went inside and found Neil setting water glasses at two place settings. He'd made mozzarella, basil, and tomato sandwiches on fresh-baked focaccia. Sunflowers, purple coneflowers, and black-eyed Susans—no doubt straight from the garden—bloomed in vases on the table and counter. A mixed-greens salad sat in a wooden bowl in the middle of the table.

"This is lovely." Hannah realized that she was starving. She had been too distracted to eat anything at coffee hour.

"I hope they taste good, but I'm afraid I'm going to have to take mine to go," Neil said. "I need to get to the store."

"I thought you were going to check out the insulation at the cottage today," Lacy said.

"I was, but duty calls. There was a mix-up with one of my recent book deliveries, and I need to go straighten it out and update my inventory before we open again on Tuesday. I'm sorry, sweetheart." Neil wrapped his own sandwich in wax paper and put it inside a plastic bag.

"No need to be sorry," Lacy said. "Thanks for making lunch. I'll take care of dinner."

He leaned in and gave her a kiss on the cheek. "And I'll check on the cottage this week, I promise." He hurried out the door.

"You're working on the cottage?" Hannah asked.

"Yeah, we were talking last night and decided that if we're ever going to convince Mom to move into it, we need to update the plumbing and electricity and all that."

"Fixing up the place is a nice idea," Hannah said.

"An expensive one, though," Lacy said. "It will take us quite a while, but we figure in the end it will be better than having her pay rent to live someplace else. And we'd love to have her nearby if there are grandchildren someday. It would be a big help."

"No kidding." Hannah felt a pang of fresh grief, realizing that her mother would never get to meet her kids, if she ever had any.

"Anyway, fixing up the cottage is a problem for another day. For now, let's eat."

After they blessed the meal, Lacy told Hannah about her conversation with Ryder and Liam.

"So you owe Liam a peach pie?" Lacy raised an eyebrow.

"That's hardly the point I was trying to make," Hannah said. "The point is that they don't think there's anything in the hills around town that the keys could unlock."

"So the hill thing is a dead end."

"That angle is. I'm sure it means something. We just don't know what yet. What was your idea?"

"Well, it doesn't have anything to do with mountains, so it may be another dead end," Lacy said. "But I was thinking about why someone would go to the trouble of sending my mom and me nearly matching keys, and I was thinking that someone wanted us to work together on something."

"Seems like a logical conclusion."

"The one thing we've been disagreeing about—the thing someone might want us to solve—is her living situation. She lived on this farm for so long, and I've lived on it for most of my life too. It would make sense for the keys to unlock something on this farm, don't you think?"

"It's definitely a possibility," Hannah said. "So, do you want to go around trying locks on the farm and see if anything opens?"

"Well, not every lock. There are some that are too new to fit the keys, so it won't be them."

"Okay." Hannah took a bite of her sandwich. "Are there any lockable doors on the farm that you don't have a key to?"

"Well, no." Lacy pressed her lips together. "But maybe there are two keys that open one of the locks? Maybe it's a skeleton key, and it opens multiple locks."

"We might as well test it out," Hannah said. "After we eat."

When they were done eating and cleaning the kitchen, they headed out, Lacy's key grasped firmly in her hand. First they went around to all the exterior doors to the house, but the key didn't fit any of the locks. Lacy then tried it in the padlock on the barn doors and each of the storage areas and sheds.

"The only place left is the cottage," Lacy said.

"Let's try it then." Hannah was skeptical, but she couldn't deny that she was interested in seeing the cottage. It wouldn't hurt to take a walk out there.

Lacy started back to her truck.

"We're not walking?" Hannah asked.

"We could," Lacy said. "There's a path that goes through the trees. But it's much faster to drive."

Hannah shrugged and climbed in beside Lacy, who backed out of the driveway and turned onto the road and then immediately onto a long dirt driveway. They bounced down the drive, and

Hannah saw a white clapboard house surrounded by tall trees. A gutter hung loose, one of the windows was cracked, and there was a chain and padlock on the front door. A stream burbled behind it, and what must have once been a beautiful garden now sat overgrown and choked with weeds.

"You might need to do some cleanup before your mom could move in," Hannah said.

"But wouldn't it be nice, once that was done?" Lacy said. "This place could be so cute."

They walked up to the front door, and Lacy tried the key in the padlock and then the door lock. "No dice," she said, shaking her head.

"I mean, it would be kind of strange if it had worked, wouldn't it?" Hannah said. "Someone sent you those keys, and who could it have been if the keys had worked here? Neil?"

Lacy shook her head. "I guess you're right. It doesn't make a ton of sense. Neil told me last night that he had nothing to do with it. He even called his parents, and they're stumped as well."

"I don't see who it could have been," Hannah said.

"Yeah, well, let's scratch that idea off the list," Lacy said. "I have another idea, though."

"What's that?"

"There's a bunch of stuff in the attic. I don't go up there very often, but last time I was up there, I saw a few chests. I wonder if these keys open one of those."

"Let's try it." This idea seemed a bit more likely to Hannah than the keys opening random buildings on the farm. They drove back to the house.

Lacy led the way upstairs. Hannah held on to the banister, worn smooth through years of use. Lacy's childhood bedroom was at the front of the house, and the rooms Lacy's parents had used as an office and a guest room were at the back.

Lacy pulled the string on a hatch in the ceiling and then unfolded a set of rickety stairs. "Be careful," she said, starting up. "The rungs are very narrow."

Her friend climbed with care. Hannah followed and soon stepped into a dim, dusty room with raw wooden floors and ceilings. The gables and eaves made the room's height uneven, but it was a vast space. Lacy tugged a string on a lightbulb, and a dim yellow glow lit the room.

Hannah took in the furniture covered with sheets, stacks of boxes and chests, bookcases stuffed full of books, and random assortments of things on every surface. She spotted a set of tartan-print luggage that was probably from the fifties, a metal washtub and washboard, a box labeled OBSOLETE ELECTRONICS, and a shelf of leather-bound encyclopedias. She could see out over the cornfields through the window directly in front of her.

"This is incredible." She stepped forward and eyed a framed map that leaned against a dresser partly covered by a dusty sheet. "This map has the USSR on it."

"I should take that down to show Neil. He loves old maps."

"Amazing." Hannah regarded a dress form with a half-finished blue wool dress pinned to it. "There are all kinds of fascinating things up here."

"You're right," Lacy said. "It's a bit overwhelming at the same time. Someone will have to clean this out at some point. How am I supposed to know what's worth keeping and what's not?"

"This is definitely worth keeping." Hannah had donned a stiff felt hat in a bright blue with a purple ribbon around the crown and fine netting along the brim. "I don't understand why you're not already wearing this to church."

Lacy chuckled. "It would certainly attract attention."

Hannah returned the hat to the coatrack where she'd found it and followed Lacy as she moved through the rows of boxes to a group of trunks lined up against what must have been the back of the house, judging by the lack of gables on that side. There was an elaborate steamer chest edged with tooled leather and brass fittings, a travel trunk with leather straps, and a plain wooden chest finished in a high-gloss varnish.

"I think the key might open this one," Lacy said, indicating the steamer trunk, which had a built-in lock. "I don't know what happened to the key that went with it, but it isn't here. I searched everywhere."

"This looks promising," Hannah said.

Lacy took the key out of her pocket and tried it in the trunk's lock, but it didn't fit. "I don't think this is it," she said, her voice edged with disappointment.

"Maybe it fits one of the others?" Hannah said.

Lacy tried the lock on the leather travel trunk, but it didn't fit there either. "This trunk is unlocked anyway," Lacy said, lifting the lid. "And the wooden one doesn't even have a lock."

Hannah peered inside the leather trunk. It was piled with clothes.

"They're my mother's, mostly from when she was a teenager, going by all the polyester and fringe. I don't know why they saved it at all, let alone in that fancy trunk."

Hannah crouched for a closer look at the lock on the steamer trunk. It seemed like a standard barrel lock, but it was hard to tell. "Do you have any idea what's in here?" It would take some work to get it open, and she didn't want to bother if it was merely old clothes.

"I thought it might have Mom's papers and things, but I don't know for sure. We had movers pack up my grandma's house after she died."

"And they didn't send a key?"

"If they did, it got lost in the transition. Mom probably would have tracked it down back then, but that was right when Dad first got sick, and she didn't have the time or the brain space, I guess. Or maybe it felt like too much, going through her mom's things after she passed. All I know is that it came from my grandma's house and we've never opened it."

"Well, I can try to get it open, but no promises."

"How would you get it open without a key?"

Hannah spotted a thin wire coat hanger. "I dealt with a finicky lock on an office door at one of the restaurants I worked at in California. It got expensive to keep calling the locksmith, so I got good at picking it." She unhooked the thin metal and placed one end into the bottom of the lock. She slid the other end into the lock and used it to press up on the tumblers inside.

"You're saying you can pick locks now? I knew you changed while you were in California, but I didn't realize it had gone to that level."

"Not everyone who can pick locks is a criminal mastermind. And I can't pick all kinds of locks. But this one seems like something I might be able to get open." She used one wire to press the lever while feeling for the pins with the other wire. There was the first stiff pin. She pressed it up until it clicked into place.

"Why didn't you replace the lock on the office door?" Lacy asked.

"The owner didn't want to. I don't know why. It wasn't my decision, but it became my problem, so I got good at this." She felt the next stiff pin and pressed it up until it clicked into place. "I think it's working." It only took a few more minutes before she felt the final pin press into place and the lock clicked open. "There we go."

"You're a genius, Hannah."

Hannah pulled the wire out of the lock and set it down, and then she lifted the lid of the trunk.

"Oh wow," Lacy said. "What is all this stuff?"

Chapter Six

The chest was packed full of papers and journals and photographs and who knew what all. Hannah reached in and took out a yearbook. *McKinley High School 1956* was emblazoned across the cover in green lettering. "Check this out."

Lacy flipped open the yearbook, thumbed through it, and then pointed to a photo of a young woman in a white, collared shirt. Her dark hair was pinned up in rolls, and she wore a silver necklace with a small cross pendant. The name under the photo read *Helen Whitmore*. "That's my grandma."

"I met her a couple times when she came to visit." Hannah gazed at the photo. "She was quite pretty." She noted that all the students on the page were seniors.

"Grandma was tough as nails. She looks sweet here, and she was, but she was also not about to let me get away with anything."

"I also remember that," Hannah said. "One time we were out playing with the kittens in the barn, and she told us to wash our hands before we could have some of the cookies she'd made. We washed them, but when she found out we hadn't used the nail brush to scrub under our nails, she sent us back and made us do it again. I'd never even seen a nail brush before that day."

"I remember that. I thought she was so mean. And then the cookies had raisins, but they looked like chocolate chips, which was doubly disappointing."

"I don't remember the cookies, only that I was a little scared of your grandma," Hannah said.

Lacy laughed. "I mean, she wasn't wrong. Those barn cats are crawling with germs. It probably was smart to have us make sure our hands were truly clean." She ran a finger over the photo. "It's funny to see her so young."

"Where is McKinley High?" Hannah asked.

"Eastern Kentucky. Harlan County, I guess. That's where she was originally from." Lacy gazed at the photo for a moment longer before setting it down. "Let's see what else is in here." Digging through, they found folders of important papers, an envelope full of cards—birthday, Christmas, and thank-you notes—that had been given to Christine by someone named Marilyn. Judging by the ages and images printed on the cards, they had been sent when Christine was a child.

"Who is Marilyn?" Hannah asked.

"I think that was Mom's godmother," Lacy said. "Marilyn Pierson, Grandma's best friend. She's probably in the yearbook too. They grew up together." Lacy opened the yearbook again and found the picture of Marilyn, a girl with round cheeks, a big smile, and long, light hair.

"Is she still around?" Hannah asked.

"That is a very good question. I don't think so, but Mom would know for sure. I met her a couple times when I was young." Lacy sat back on her heels. "You're thinking that because her name starts with *M*, aren't you?"

"I'm merely suggesting that maybe we should learn more about her," Hannah said.

"Not a bad idea. We should call my mom anyway to tell her what's in here." Lacy pulled her phone out of her pocket and called Christine. "Voice mail," she mouthed to Hannah, and then, into the phone, said, "Hi, Mom. Hannah managed to get one of these old chests open in the attic. It's got stuff we thought you'd like to see. Give me a call or feel free to stop on by if you're around." She ended the call. "In the meantime, let's see what else is in here."

Lacy reached into the chest and pushed aside pieces of crumpled newspaper to reveal a stack of leather-bound journals. Hannah picked up the top one and flipped it open. *Helen Frances Whitmore, 1955* was written in blue ink on the first page.

The pages were filled with neat, precise handwriting in faded blue ink. Hannah studied the handwriting and quickly decided it hadn't been written by the same person who had composed the poem. That writing was spidery and thin, while these letters were perfectly formed and evenly lined up. It also didn't match the writing on the envelopes either. Even if her writing had changed as she'd gotten older, it appeared as though this had been penned by a totally different person. She flipped through a couple of pages and saw that Helen had journaled faithfully, chronicling her days even when there wasn't much to report. That explained why there were dozens of these journals in the trunk. There wasn't time to go through them now.

"Do you think anything in here might help with the mystery?" Hannah asked.

"I don't see how," Lacy said. "Grandma passed some years ago, so I don't think she could have sent the packages."

"Seems unlikely." Hannah hoisted out a stack of the journals and set them aside.

Lacy withdrew a couple of stacks of letters—one large pile from Walter Knicely, Lacy's grandfather, and another bunch from someone named Bert Meisel. "Who is Bert?" Lacy asked, opening one of the envelopes. She unfolded a letter and started reading. "Oh wow. These are love letters from 1955. It looks like Bert wrote to my grandmother from college in Boston."

"That's sweet."

Lacy shook her head and slipped the letter back into the envelope. "Sorry, Bert, she married someone else."

"I wonder what happened between the two of them," Hannah said.

"I have no idea," Lacy said, "but I'll have fun going through those, I'm sure."

"When did she meet your grandfather?"

"They grew up together. Their fathers were both miners, and they lived in the company town."

"Could this Bert guy have anything to do with the handkerchiefs? His last name, Meisel, starts with *M*, and he's from a time when they would have used handkerchiefs."

"I mean, I guess it's a possibility. But how would he know Mom's address or mine?"

"To be fair, your address is on the farm's website and social media. Perhaps your mom has hers online somewhere as well."

Lacy picked up the stack of letters. "I'll read through these, in case there's something here."

Hannah reached back in and found a framed photo of Helen and a man who must have been Walter standing in front of a church. Helen wore a knee-length white dress, and Walter wore a dark suit.

"Wedding photo?" Hannah said, holding it up.

"Aw, they were so happy. And so young."

Hannah handed the frame to Lacy, who opened it to reveal a few loose photographs beneath, also from the wedding. They were formal portraits of the families—one of Lacy's grandpa with his parents and two brothers, and one of Helen's family, with her parents and—

"Who's this?" Hannah pointed to a girl with light hair and a wistful smile standing next to Helen.

"Oh, that's Grandma's sister, Nancy. They didn't get along. I don't think I ever met her."

"That's sad. What happened? Is she still around?"

"No idea. Grandma didn't talk about her. Maybe Mom would know."

Looking at the piles of things they'd unearthed from the chest, Hannah wasn't confident there was much of anything to help them with their mystery. There were no more handkerchiefs. No poems that she could see. No keys, and nothing to unlock.

But they had a few leads. Lacy would read the letters from Bert Meisel, and as soon as they heard from Christine, they would ask about her godmother, Marilyn.

It was a start. But it still felt like they were a very long way from finding answers.

Hannah's apartment was stifling when she returned from Lacy's farm that afternoon. She cranked up the window AC units, changed out of her church dress into shorts and a T-shirt, and made herself an iced coffee.

She read while she drank the coffee then tossed in a load of laundry. She called Amos Bowers and made an appointment for him to come by the following afternoon. She set a pot of water on to boil and started chopping tomatoes. Hannah had stopped at a farm stand on the way home and bought some ripe heirloom tomatoes, fresh basil, and homemade mozzarella cheese. They would become a simple supper of pasta and a sauce made from the tomatoes, basil, and some good olive oil, with fresh cheese on top. Just because she was cooking for one didn't mean she couldn't eat well.

As she was about to toss the orecchiette into the water, her phone rang. Lacy.

"Hey," she said, pinning the phone between her shoulder and her ear.

"Hey. Mom stopped by and I showed her what we found in the trunk. She loved seeing so many of Grandma's old things, and some of her own too."

"I bet she did. It's cool to see so many parts of your grandma's life."

"I also asked her about Marilyn, her godmother, but she told me Marilyn died a long time ago."

"That's too bad."

"It is. Mom said she was a lovely woman. She lived in eastern Kentucky, but came to visit all the time when Mom was a kid. But she died twenty-five years ago."

"It's unlikely those packages were sent by her then." Hannah carefully poured pasta into the water. "Did you learn anything about your grandma's sister?"

"Nothing. Mom doesn't know anything about her or why they fell out. She doesn't even remember meeting her."

"Did she think that's odd, never knowing her mother's sister?"

"Sure, now, but that's the kind of thing you accept as a kid, right? Apparently she asked about it once, but her mom brushed the question aside and she never asked again. She wishes she knew more now, but in any case, Mom doesn't think she would have anything to do with this whole thing. Nancy was not a figure in her life and probably doesn't even know I exist, so I don't think that's likely to go anywhere."

"And Bert?"

"Mom never heard of him, but I'll read some of the letters tonight and see what they can tell us."

After they hung up, Hannah read some more of her book while she ate her dinner, which came out fresh and tasting like summer. She cleaned up the kitchen and got ready for bed, her mind swirling, but no closer to finding answers.

It wasn't until she was tossing and turning in the middle of the night that she had an idea. It was probably a long shot, but—well, she would investigate tomorrow.

After a restless night, Hannah slept in Monday morning, and she woke to find sunlight streaming in through the big windows of her apartment. It was going to be another hot, sunny day, and she was grateful for the air-conditioning that kept her apartment cool.

She sat at the table with coffee, a bagel, and her Bible and read from 1 Corinthians. She was on chapter 13 and almost skipped the passage entirely. The famous love chapter. She'd heard it at a hundred weddings, and love was not what she wanted to read about when she was definitely not interested in dating.

But she read it anyway, forcing herself to slow down and not rush past the familiar words—love is patient, love is kind, it does not envy, it does not boast, it is not proud—and really take in what true love for another person looked like. The Bible didn't specify this was only for romantic love, after all. This was supposed to apply to all love.

But then she got closer to the end of the passage, and read some also-familiar verses that were often overlooked in this passage. "For now we see only a reflection as in a mirror; then we shall see face to face. Now I know in part; then I shall know fully, even as I am fully known." It was a good reminder that she couldn't see everything yet. That God had a plan, and she had to trust Him to reveal it in time.

Hannah had planned to spend a good chunk of the day at the restaurant, catching up on invoicing and bills and calling local distributors, before going to see Amos Bowers about his beef and then to dinner at Drew and Allison's. But after the restless night she'd had, she knew she needed to start by investigating the idea that had come to her before bed.

After she'd cleaned up the kitchen, she called Lacy, who got up with the chickens.

"Hi. Are you busy today?" Hannah asked when Lacy picked up.

"Sadly, I am, at least this morning. I have this enormous egg order for a new restaurant in town."

"I suppose I can't complain about that." She would need to accept the delivery when Lacy came by.

On the other end of the line, Hannah heard the chicken coop door creaking closed as her friend chuckled. "Why?"

"I had an idea last night. The key. Like, a map key." As she laid in bed, she'd been turning the word *key* over in her mind and had thought of a map key. She didn't know how the square on a map that explained what the symbols meant had anything to do with the physical keys, but once the idea had lodged in her mind, she couldn't shake it.

"What about a map key?"

"What if the keys have something to do with maps?"

"It's possible." Lacy sounded skeptical.

"Okay, now that I say it out loud, it doesn't sound as genius as it did to me at two a.m." It sounded like kind of a stretch, if she was honest.

"I don't see what one would have to do with the other, but I guess it can't hurt to check it out. And I know just the person to help you—Neil."

"I thought that too." In addition to books, Neil's store stocked an interesting selection of antique maps and atlases. Neil loved maps. If there was a connection to a map here, he would find it. "I know you've told him about the handkerchiefs and keys—"

"But I didn't ask him to think of them in the context of maps. Maybe it will shake something loose." A creak sounded as Lacy closed the chicken coop door again. "Are you sure you're not using this as an excuse to buy more books?"

"Would you complain even if I was?" Hannah teased. "You know I'm passionate about supporting small businesses."

"I guess not. Feel free to spend as much as you want at my husband's store."

"Thanks. Good luck with the chickens."

Hannah got dressed and ready for the day, and then she walked the few blocks to the bookshop. The air was hot and thick, and she was sweating by the time she got to the store.

She stepped inside, and the wave of cool air that washed over her felt heavenly. The walls were lined with shelves packed with hardcovers and paperbacks, and more shelving ran the length of the store. There was a small seating area with two wingback chairs in front of a fireplace, above which hung an antique map of Blackberry Valley. A small children's area was located in the back, complete with beanbag chairs, while display tables piled with bestsellers encouraged adults to browse.

Even though Hannah hadn't intended to come in here to shop, she couldn't keep from picking up a book with great reviews. The cover had a picture of an old English manor house set in the rolling countryside, but the description suggested that something sinister had happened at the house, and its new resident, a veterinarian, was determined to find out what it was. The cool English countryside sounded delicious in this heat.

"Hi, Hannah," Neil said, emerging from the rear of the shop. "How are you?"

"I'm doing well, except that you've already made me spend money I didn't intend to spend." She held up the book.

"That's a good one. And it's way cheaper than a trip to Yorkshire."

"What can I do? I can't fight logic like that." Whenever she was tempted to feel bad about spending money on books, Hannah remembered how her mother had often said buying books was always money well-spent. Books could take the reader to new worlds, show them places they might never visit in real life, and introduce them to characters who became friends—all for the price of a few cups of coffee. "I'll take it. But that's not why I came in here."

"What did you come for?"

"To ask you a question that sounded great at two a.m., but now sounds a bit strange."

Neil's eyes lit up. "With an introduction like that, I can't wait."

His enthusiasm encouraged Hannah. "You know the keys Lacy and Christine received in the mail? I wondered if there might be any connection to a map key."

"How so?" Neil asked.

"Like, could the mountain symbol on the keys correlate to the symbol for mountains on a map somewhere? And if we could find the right map, the one that has that symbol, maybe it would lead us to whatever these keys unlock." Hearing her own words, Hannah grimaced. "I told you it sounded better at two a.m."

"I wouldn't say that. Do you have the keys?" Neil asked. "Lacy showed me hers, but I'd love to see it again."

"I have a photo of them." Hannah opened the picture on her phone and handed it over.

Neil zoomed in on the ornate head. "This symbol is familiar to me, and I can't remember why." He glanced at the photo again. "It would make sense. It could be the symbol for a mountain on a map key." He gestured for her to follow him. "Come with me."

She left the book on the counter and followed him down a long aisle between the shelves to the small area at the rear of the shop devoted to antique maps. There was a wooden table with a bin of maps in plastic sleeves, backed by cardboard.

He tugged one out of the bin. "This map shows the main industry in each region of the state, circa 1930." It showed the outline of the state of Kentucky, but instead of labeling the cities and roads, it was marked with little symbols that showed a stalk of grain, a tree, a fish, and a pickax, among others.

Hannah leaned forward to find Blackberry Valley on the map. The area around the town was labeled with a stalk of grain, which meant agriculture was the main industry around here. That sounded right. She studied the map's key and saw that the other symbols represented logging, fishing, mining—all industries that had driven the economy in Kentucky.

"This isn't what you're looking for exactly," Neil said. "But I was thinking of something like this, where a mountain symbol might represent hills and a water symbol might represent rivers or lakes."

"Do you have a map like that?"

"Not off the top of my head, but I'll dig through my collection to be sure. The symbol is familiar, so maybe it's on one of the maps I have around here somewhere."

"I appreciate it," Hannah said.

"I'll let you know if I find anything," Neil said.

They started toward the front of the shop, and in the process walked past the poetry section of the store, which sparked an idea.

"Did Lacy show you the poem Christine got in her package?" Hannah asked.

"She did," Neil said. "It's too bad it got wet. It's nearly impossible to read."

Hannah pulled up the photo she'd taken of the poem. The photo itself was kind of blurry, and it was hard to make out more than a few words. *Long years... cannot fill— The absence... -and years. They were fire—And understand—.*

"I was wondering if it was an original poem or a famous poem that's too smeared to recognize."

"You're welcome to peruse the poetry section," he said, gesturing in the direction they'd come from. "If it's a poem I've read before, I can't remember it." He gazed at the photo on her screen. "Maybe if the picture was a bit clearer, that would help. Or if I saw it in real life, maybe I could make out more than I can on the screen." He shook his head. "Another reason it would be great if Christine lived on the property."

"Lacy was mentioning that the other day, how her mom doesn't want to live on the farm anymore."

"I don't understand it," Neil said. "I mean, I guess I could see not wanting to live in the house with us, since she lived there for so long with her late husband. And I understand wanting her own space. But the cottage solves both of those problems. It's free, and it's so close, and it's right on the land where she lived most of her life. She always talks about how she misses waking up to the rooster's crow and being surrounded by cornfields, but when we bring it up, she says she doesn't want to move back."

"The cottage does need some work," Hannah said, remembering the peeling paint and the sagging gutter. "I can see why she might not want to move there yet."

"We would fix it up," Neil said. "It will take some time to save up enough to make it really nice, but we could get it habitable pretty easily. She wouldn't have to do a thing. But she doesn't want to, and I don't understand why."

"I'm sure she has her reasons," Hannah said. "Maybe she likes the change of pace, living in town."

"If you talk to her, she doesn't seem to," Neil said with a shrug. "Anyway, my point is that I haven't seen the actual paper with the poem itself, but maybe if you did, it would be easier to read and identify?"

"Maybe." Hannah had seen the original, and it hadn't rung any bells. Perhaps if she saw it again... "I'll see if Christine will let me take another look. In the meantime, I'll take this." She indicated the book on the counter.

"Sure thing." Neil ducked behind the counter and rang up the book. "Thanks for coming in. And I'll let you know if I come up with anything with that mountain."

"Thank you." Hannah stepped out into the heat, and she found Christine's number and gave her a call.

"Hi, Hannah," Christine said. "Are you calling with good news?"

"It's not bad news, if that counts for anything."

"I'll take it."

"I was wondering if I could come and see that poem again. The picture I have is blurry, and I wondered if I might be able to make out more if I saw the original."

"Sure. If you can figure out what it means, you're doing better than I am. I'll be here until about noon if you want to stop by today. My apartment is over the stationery store."

"I do. Can I come in a few minutes?"

"I'll be here."

As Hannah set off down the sidewalk, she reflected that it wasn't as if anyone could accuse her of being unproductive on her day off.

Chapter Seven

Hannah decided to make a quick stop at Jump Start Coffee before her visit with Christine, and she smiled when she saw Zane Forrest behind the register. Zane was the brother of the Hot Spot's chef, though he was generally more laid-back than Jacob. Today he wore a rumpled button-down with khaki shorts, and he had several days' worth of scruff on his chin.

"Hi, Hannah," he said. "What can I get for you?"

"An iced coffee, please."

"Funny enough, those are really popular today."

"On a day like today? Weird," she joked. The air-conditioning kept the shop cool, but she'd gotten hot again on the short walk over. As much as she loved summer, the humidity made it hard to tolerate sometimes. "And I'll take one of those blueberry muffins as well." She wanted to take something to Christine.

"Coming right up." Moments later, he held out a to-go cup in one hand, the bagged muffin in the other.

"Thank you." She took both, and the cool condensation on the outside of the cup felt heavenly as she headed for the door.

Outside, she made her way to the stationery store, with its charming display of cards and cheery wrapping paper in the window. Through the glass, she saw a set of wooden stairs leading to the apartment above, much like the door to her own apartment. She pressed the buzzer, and when the door buzzed, she pushed it open and climbed up the stairs. The stairs and hallway were scuffed and dingy, and the paint was a dirty grayish color. Her footsteps echoed as she made her way up the steps.

"Hi." Christine was waiting with the door open when Hannah reached the second floor. "Twice in one week. I feel downright lucky."

"Thank you so much for letting me stop by. I hoped I might be able to make out more of the poem if I saw it again in person. Like, maybe there's a trace of ink on the paper that doesn't show up in the photo."

"You're welcome to take another look."

"I brought you a muffin." Hannah held out the bag. "I didn't know how you like your coffee, but I can go back and grab something if you'd like."

"Don't be silly. I've already had my coffee today. Please come in and make yourself at home."

Christine stepped aside to allow Hannah to enter the small living room. Hannah hadn't been there before, so she was surprised at the wave of nostalgia that washed over her when she stepped inside. Though the room was smaller than the family room at the farm, it held the same sofa she and Lacy had lounged on as teenagers. Christine's recliner occupied one corner, her ever-present bag of knitting on the floor beside it. Hannah's heart constricted when she saw the bigger recliner that Lacy's father had favored in the opposite corner. A family portrait hung above the couch, six-year-old Lacy's grin unchanged by the decades. A flat-screen television had replaced the heavy tube that had been old-fashioned even then, but otherwise she could have been back on the farm.

"What a cozy room," she said to Christine. "It's so welcoming."

"Thank you. I've tried to make it feel like home."

There was something unsaid beneath her words that Hannah wasn't sure she wanted to probe. Luckily, there wasn't time to ponder it, as Christine gestured for Hannah to follow her through a doorway into the small but well-appointed kitchen.

"Thanks again for agreeing to a visit on such short notice."

"Oh, sweetheart, I'm not doing a thing but watching game shows on the television. There's not much to do here in town, so I'm happy to have a visitor. Have a seat." She gestured to a small wooden table with two chairs. These were new, as Lacy had the old table and chairs at the farm.

Again, Hannah wasn't sure if there was a subtext she was supposed to be picking up on. Most people would have said there was a lot more to do in town than out at the farm, and it sure sounded like Christine was hinting at something. But it wasn't her place to open that door, and she decided to focus on the task at hand.

Hannah slid into a chair at the kitchen table. The padded envelope sat in the middle, and she reached for it, while Christine set the muffin on a small plate. It was from the same set—white Corelle rimmed with green flowers—that she'd used when Hannah and Lacy were kids.

Christine sat in the chair across from Hannah as she opened the envelope and removed the handkerchief, the key, and finally the poem. "Lacy called and asked me about my godmother, Marilyn.

But she passed so long ago that I don't see how she could have been involved with this."

"It would require a pretty elaborate plan for the envelopes to have been sent to you now, twenty-five years after she passed," Hannah agreed. "She would really be playing the long game."

"Lacy also asked about a man my mother wrote to while he was in college, but I don't see how a man I've never heard of could be involved in this. I keep thinking the M might mean Neil is involved somehow, but Lacy insists he's not."

"He was genuinely confused by this whole thing when I talked to him earlier this morning."

"If Frank were here, he would have some good ideas. Frank was always clever like that."

"I'm sorry. It must be hard to be without him for so long."

"It's funny to go from spending every day of your life with someone to not having them there anymore," Christine said wistfully. "We were together for more than forty years."

"How did you meet?" Hannah realized she had never heard the story, and it seemed to be one Christine wanted to tell.

"We met on the first day of college," Christine said with a smile. "I was trying to find my English classroom, and Frank came by and helped me. Turned out he was in the same class, and he sat next to me. I suggested we go out for ice cream later so I could thank him, and that was that."

"Where did you go to college?" How did Hannah not know this?

"University of Kentucky," Christine said. "I was studying to be a nurse, and he was studying agriculture. Of course he'd grown up on the farm, so he knew a lot, but he was hoping to modernize when he took it over, and he did. We got married the day after we graduated."

"That's such a sweet story. And it's kind of the dream, right? You got to skip all the bad dates and find the one for you right off the bat."

Christine beamed at her. "It was great. Plus, I commuted to school, so I sometimes feel like I didn't get the full college experience. Frank lived on campus, so I got to attend dances at his fraternity and that sort of thing."

"You commuted to college? I thought your family was from eastern Kentucky?"

"My parents were. I lived there until I was two. My dad didn't want to spend the rest of his life breathing coal dust, and my parents wanted a better life for me. They moved us to Lexington, where my dad got a factory job. Mom worked there too once I was old enough to take care of myself."

"I thought coal mining was a pretty good job back in the day."

"I guess it paid well enough, and it was all right as long as the mine didn't collapse on you and you didn't get black lung. We only went to visit a few times, so I don't know a lot about living in a mining town firsthand. What I know is that by the time I was born, it wasn't what Dad wanted. I'm proud of him for getting out."

"It must have been difficult," Hannah agreed. "Was his whole family still in that town?"

"Russell, you mean? That was the name of the company that owned the mines, so that was the name of the town. His parents both passed before I was born, but my mother's family still lived in the area, even after the mines closed. There wasn't money to go anywhere else, though my grandparents did manage to build themselves a house that was nice enough."

"You said you only visited a few times?"

"Once or twice that I remember. A trip like that would take money and time, two things my parents didn't have. And my grandparents both passed when I was still a kid—my grandma when I was thirteen, and Grandpa a few years before that—so after that there wasn't any point."

Hannah could imagine what it must have been like to leave it all behind—the town, their families, the only lives they'd known—and move to a new city to start over. It wasn't that different from what Hannah had done when she'd picked up and moved to California for college. She'd started a whole new life and loved it even though it was totally different than what she'd had. Or maybe *because* it was totally different from her childhood. And yet, here she was, back home again.

"Anyway, the first time I came to Blackberry Valley with Frank to meet his parents, I saw the farm, and I knew I was home. That farm was where I was meant to live. I knew it in my bones. I'd known Frank was the one before then, but there was no doubt in my mind after that visit."

"You truly loved living at the farm," Hannah murmured.

"It's heaven on earth."

"Yet you wouldn't want to move back?"

"It's Lacy's farm now," Christine said, her tone firm. "Lacy and Neil need the freedom to make it their own. I don't want to be in the way."

Hannah didn't want to meddle, but it almost sounded to her as if Lacy and her mom wanted the same thing without realizing it. "Have you talked to Lacy about it?"

"I can hardly invite myself back. That would be so rude. It's probably best this way, anyway."

Hannah decided not to say anything to Christine, but would mention it to Lacy. For now, she picked up the heavy bronze key and turned it over in her hands, studying the mountain design. Seeing it up close didn't show her anything that wasn't in the picture.

She moved on to the handkerchief, which was as she remembered. The *M* embroidered in blue thread, the stitches uneven, the letter crooked. Had a child done it?

She set it down and slid the poem over to her.

Long years... cannot fill—
The absence...

Up close, it almost looked like the next line read *Embers of a thousand years*. What did that mean?

And then the lines she already had:

They were fire
And understand

"That probably doesn't help very much, does it?" Christine asked.

"I can make out a few more words," Hannah said. "I guess we'll see. Maybe those new words will shake something loose. It's not *un*helpful."

She picked up the padded envelope and flipped it over in her hands. Where had this come from? Who had sent it and why? She studied the writing, hoping to make out some clue from the hand-writing, the pen, the return address, anything. None of it was strange on the surface. The envelope was addressed to Christine, the return address was Lacy's, and—

"Wait." How had they not seen this before? "Christine, look at this."

"What is it?" Christine leaned over and looked at the top right corner of the envelope, where Hannah pointed.

"I can't believe we didn't see this before." Hannah wanted to smack herself. How had they not noticed?

"There's no postmark," Christine said. There were two stamps in the corner, but they hadn't been canceled. There was no date, time, or place stamped on them. "Is Lacy's like that?"

"I don't know." Hannah grabbed her phone and called Lacy, who picked up on the third ring.

"Hey," Lacy said.

"Hi. I'm here with your mom—"

"Hi, Lacy," Christine called.

"Oh. Uh, hi, Mom."

"I came over to take another look at the poem in her envelope, and we noticed something. There's no postmark on the envelope she received. Is there one on yours?"

"That's a great question. It's inside." A squeaky hinge groaned. "Get back in there, you silly creature. Hang on. Eggatha got out. She's almost—ha! Got you." There was the sound of a gate closing, and then heavy footsteps. "Okay. I'm heading to see."

"Is Eggatha safe?" Hannah asked.

"She's in the coop, so she's safe for now. But if she tries that again, she might find herself being made into chicken soup."

Hannah laughed. Eggatha was one of Lacy's favorite chickens and was in no danger.

"All right, let me see." A second later, she gasped. "There's no postmark. But that means it wasn't mailed."

"That seems to be the logical conclusion," Hannah agreed.

"Then how did I get it?"

"It must have been hand-delivered," Christine said.

"Lacy, I saw you take your mail out of the mailbox," Hannah said, trying to get it all straight in her head. "It was there with the other mail, but I suppose that doesn't mean it was dropped off by the post office. Someone could have come along and stuck it in the mailbox after the mail truck went by."

"They must have," Lacy said.

"Where is your mail delivered?" Hannah asked Christine.

"It gets slid through the mail slot in the door that leads to the street," Christine said. "I scoop it up from there. The envelope was lying there on the floor with the other mail, so I assumed it was delivered with the rest of it, but maybe it wasn't. I suppose anyone could have slid the envelope through the mail slot."

"I suppose neither one of you has a security camera?"

"No," Lacy said.

"Nope," Christine said. "But maybe the stationery store does? I don't know."

"It would be great to see who dropped off the envelopes," Hannah said. "At least one of the businesses on this block must have security cameras. We'll start asking."

Hannah didn't have time to go door-to-door asking about whether any of the shops had security camera footage, as much as she wanted to. She was supposed to meet Amos Bowers at his farm in twenty minutes, and it would take nearly that long to drive there.

She hurried to her apartment, where her car was parked, and unlocked the driver's side door. As she was climbing in, a short beep sounded from her phone, announcing the arrival of a text message. It was from Liam "The Hero" Berthold.

JUST CHECKING IN ON WHEN I'M GOING TO GET THAT PEACH PIE, he wrote, followed by a smiley face emoji.

Hannah quickly texted him back. THESE THINGS TAKE TIME. AND PEACHES, APPARENTLY. BUT YOU'LL GET IT SOON, I PROMISE.

After tossing her phone in the cupholder and starting the car, she pointed the vents directly at her face as the cool air started pouring out.

Amos Bower showed Hannah around his farm, and she was pleased to see that he ran a clean, efficient, and humane operation. She told him how much beef she would need, and they agreed on a price. She was on her way in no time.

On the way to town, she stopped at Hubbard's Orchard, returning to the Hot Spot with five bushels of ripe, fragrant fresh peaches a little while later. She wouldn't need all of them to make Liam's pie, of course, but she would also make one to bring to dinner at Drew and Allison's tonight.

She lost herself in making two peach pies—rolling out and chilling the dough, peeling the peaches, sprinkling on sugar and a hint of cinnamon.

While the pies baked, she made a key ingredient for her new twist on Kentucky Hot Browns. It was unconventional, to be sure, but as she boiled blackberries into a compote, she truly believed it would taste amazing. As much as she loved the hum and activity of the restaurant when it was busy, there was something soothing about being home alone, seeing the place she had built and having it all to herself, trying new things.

An hour later, the compote was cooling, and the golden-brown pies released a heavenly aroma. She would try to find out whether there was any security footage from the businesses near Christine's place tomorrow. Hopefully any potential recordings would show who had delivered the packages. That, at least, would be a good start.

But for now, dinner.

Chapter Eight

Hannah parked behind her father's vehicle in the driveway of Drew and Allison's charming two-story home. They'd bought the old Federal-style house ten years before, and it had been in various stages of renovation ever since. The building was a simple rectangular brick box with three-part Palladian windows on either side of the front door and a row of symmetrical windows on the second. Last year they'd painted the shutters black to match the door, which enhanced the already stately appearance.

With a plastic pie carrier in one hand and a zippered bag of dog treats in the other, Hannah walked up the brick stairs leading to the columned portico. Before she could press the bell, the door burst open and Axel charged in her direction.

"Aunt Hannah's here," he shouted, throwing his arms around her torso. Then he noticed her dish. "What did you bring?"

"Peach pie," she told her nephew. "What else?"

He released her and stormed into the house. "She brought peach pie."

With a chuckle, Hannah followed and closed the door behind her. The sound of tapping on the polished hardwood floor in the entry hall alerted her to the approach of Zeus, her father's border terrier.

"Hey, boy," she said, bending to scratch him behind the ears. "I brought something for you too."

The dog's tail wagged like a windshield wiper in a rainstorm while she opened the baggie and withdrew a bone-shaped biscuit.

"There you go," she said, extending the treat.

Zeus took it gently from her fingers and then trotted off to the family room, tail still wagging. She heard the sounds of a video game coming from there as well.

"We're in the kitchen," Allison's voice called from a doorway at the end of the short hallway.

Hannah stuck her head into the family room to say hello to AJ, who grinned at her in greeting, and then made her way down the hall. She stopped in the doorway of the newly remodeled kitchen.

"Oh, wow." Her gaze swept the room. "This is amazing. You've done a fabulous job."

Allison turned from a shiny ceramic cooktop, wooden spoon in hand. "Thank you." She brushed a stray lock of auburn hair out of her eyes. "I'm happy with the way it came out."

Seated at a built-in booth, Ava busily arranged carrot sticks on a tray of fresh vegetables. The little girl lifted a lopsided grin in her direction. "I'm helping."

"And doing a great job too," Hannah told her. "When you're a little older, maybe you can work with me at the restaurant."

Ava preened and placed another carrot stick carefully on top of the others.

Hannah set her pie carrier on the kitchen island and ran a hand across the smooth marble surface. Her sister-in-law possessed a flair for decorating, and that talent was in full evidence in this room. A stainless-steel double-wall oven stood at one end, surrounded by pristine white cabinetry. Huge windows along the back of the house overlooked a sunny patio, where Hannah caught sight of Drew and her father at the grill.

"Barbecue chicken?" she asked.

"Right." Allison stirred a simmering pot on the stove. "And hot dogs."

"What can I do to help?"

Her hostess gestured to the sink. "Want to shuck some corn?"

"Sure." Hannah found the sink full of corn. "Boiling or grilling?"

"Grilling. Foil's in the pantry." She gestured at a door behind Ava's booth.

Hannah loved grilled corn on the cob. It retained so much flavor. After retrieving the foil and butter, she picked up an ear and stripped off the husk.

"There's a lot of corn here." She cleaned the silks from the first ear, smothered it in butter and seasonings, and wrapped foil around it. "Do you want me to shuck all of them? There's only seven of us."

"Eight," Ava piped up from the booth. "Mama told me to count eight forks and napkins."

Hannah caught the stern glance Allison directed at her daughter.

But her expression cleared when she saw Hannah watching. "Drew invited a friend. Someone from the office."

She turned away quickly. Too quickly. A suspicion began to niggle in the back of Hannah's mind.

"Oh?" She studied her sister-in-law's too-innocent profile. "Anyone I know?"

"I don't think so. Drew said he's new to the company." Drew was a computer programmer at a small company that made educational software. "I've never met him. Apparently, he moved from out of state and doesn't know many people yet."

Hannah finished wrapping another ear and set it on the counter then faced Allison. "This isn't a fix-up, is it?" She allowed her suspicions to color her tone.

Eyes wide, Allison opened her mouth to answer. The doorbell rang, and a relieved smile spread across her face. "That's probably him now. Excuse me." She hurried from the room.

Hannah left the sink to approach her niece. "Ava, what do you know about this friend of your dad's?"

The carrots were all arranged evenly on the platter, and the girl had moved on to celery sticks. "Daddy says he's perfect."

Hannah's suspicions blossomed further. "What is he perfect for, sweetie?"

"Daddy says he doesn't have a wife or kids." Ava's head tilted to one side as she considered that. "That doesn't sound perfect to me. I bet he's lonely."

Allison returned at that moment with a bouquet of brightly colored flowers. "Thank you so much, Oliver." She lifted the bouquet to her nose and inhaled. "They're beautiful."

The man who followed her through the doorway stood around the same height as Hannah's five-five. His shoulder bones protruded sharply beneath his polo shirt, and his face was thin, his cheeks hollow. He carried a second, identical bouquet.

"Please call me Ollie," he told Allison.

"Ollie, then." The smile Allison aimed at Hannah held a trace of apprehension. "And this is Hannah, Drew's sister."

"Hello, Hannah." He crossed the kitchen floor with the bouquet extended. "These are for you."

Bringing flowers to the hostess was understandable, but why bring them to another guest? The obvious answer was that the guest was a fix-up, and he knew it.

Drew, I'm going to strangle you.

She recovered herself enough to accept the offering with a smile. "Thank you, Ollie."

Zeus trotted into the room to greet the new visitor. When he sniffed Oliver's hand, the man jumped, yanking his hand away from the border terrier's scruffy snout.

"That's Zeus," Hannah said. "He's my dad's dog."

Oliver cleared his throat. "I've never quite gotten used to seeing dogs indoors."

Hannah didn't know how to respond to that. "You don't like dogs inside?"

"They're wild creatures," he said. "And full of germs, to boot."

Strike one.

Hannah met Allison's eye with a raised eyebrow.

Allison glanced away quickly. "Excuse me while I find a couple of vases." She hurried from the room.

Feeling awkward, Hannah stood still for a long moment. She became aware that Ava had stopped placing celery sticks on the tray and was staring at the newcomer.

Relieved to have something to break the silence, she introduced the child. "This is my niece, Ava." When he made no immediate reply, she added, "Drew's daughter."

A curt nod. "I've seen her picture on his desk."

He didn't look at the girl or acknowledge her, but continued to stare at Hannah. She cast about for something to say and came up empty. What was taking Allison so long?

"Are you lonely?" Ava's voice broke the awkward moment.

"I beg your pardon?"

"Daddy says you don't have any kids to play with. I would get lonely if I didn't have anybody to play with."

Ollie's lips twisted. "No. I'm not lonely." He addressed his next comment to Hannah. "I don't know if I want children of my own, personally."

Strike two. Hannah definitely wanted children someday, but more than that, it was an odd thing to lead with when speaking to a stranger. Especially in front of a child.

She set the flowers on the counter and picked up another ear of corn.

Allison returned as Hannah wrapped the cob in foil. "Here we go. These will make beautiful centerpieces on the picnic table."

"Picnic table? We're eating outdoors?"

Hannah glanced over her shoulder at the note of contempt in the man's voice. His lip curled upward.

"Well, yes." Allison cast a quick glance through the window at the patio. "It's cooled off, so I thought it would be nice to have supper on the patio."

He made no reply, though the tight line of his mouth spoke volumes about his opinion of a meal outside.

"Would you like something to drink?" Allison asked. "We have pretty much any soda you can think of, and I made a pitcher of sweet tea."

"Just water, please. I don't do sugar."

No sugar? Hannah glanced at her pie carrier. What did he mean, he didn't *do* sugar? Although, she supposed he might have diabetes and, since she wasn't about to ask the reason, she had to accept his words at face value.

"Water coming right up." Allison's voice had lost a touch of its warmth. This wasn't going well. "Maybe you'd like to join Drew and his dad on the patio."

"It was nice to meet you, Ollie," Allison said. "I'm sorry about the chicken. The next time you come, I'll be sure to have sugar-free barbecue sauce."

She and Drew stood on the front porch beside Hannah and her father to say goodbye to Oliver. How Allison managed such a friendly tone, Hannah couldn't fathom. It had taken every ounce of her strength not to bite the man's head off as he criticized every dish on the table, and she hadn't even cooked the meal.

"My food preferences are a bit eccentric by today's standards," he admitted.

A bit? Hannah swallowed a snort.

Ollie approached her and extended a hand. "I hope we can see each other again. Maybe I'll try your restaurant."

She hid behind a frozen smile. "We're open five nights a week," she managed to reply. "No reservations needed, though I'm not sure you'll find much you can eat."

He shrugged. "In that case, maybe I'll give you a call." Then, with a farewell nod at Drew and Dad, he headed for his car.

When the vehicle was safely out of earshot, Hannah rounded on her brother. "If you give that man my cell phone number, I'll never speak to you again."

"What?" Drew looked truly puzzled. "Ollie's a great guy. He's smart and has a steady job making a good salary. And he's single."

Allison folded her arms over her chest. "There's a reason he's single."

Hannah aimed a grateful smile at her then went on, "He doesn't like children. Or dogs. Or picnics. Or pretty much any food at all, although he says he doesn't have any allergies or dietary restrictions. He ate celery for supper."

Dad's head cocked sideways, considering. "That probably isn't such a good match for a woman who owns a restaurant."

"Okay," Drew admitted. "I'll give you that." His expression cleared. "There's this other guy at work who—"

Hannah held up a hand. "Nope. I'm not into blind dates, so please don't. If I want a date, I'll scare one up myself." She switched her stern stare to her father. "And I'm not interested in anyone at church either. Or anywhere else."

"Honey, we only want you to be happy," Dad told her, his voice soft.

"I am happy," she told him. "What makes you think I'm not?"

"You're alone." His words were gentle. "I hate to think of you being lonely."

"You're alone too," she pointed out. "Do you want me to start looking for a nice lady to set you up with?"

Stiffening, he said, "Of course not." He appeared slightly offended at the idea. "Besides, I'm not alone. I have Gordon."

"Your brother doesn't count," she said.

"Sure he does. That's why we live together."

Hannah laid a hand on his arm, her voice softening. "Listen, I know you love me, and I appreciate what you're trying to do. But I'm fine. Really. The restaurant takes a lot of time and effort, and I'm okay with that. That's what I want to be doing right now."

"You know what they say about all work and no play, Sis," Drew threw in.

She tilted her head and gave him a grin. "Now you're saying I'm dull?" When he started to voice a protest, she waved it off. "I have church, and friends, and all of you." She splayed her hands, indicating the three of them. "You're my family. If I get lonely, I'll call you guys. Or I'll invite the kids for a sleepover."

"That's a surefire cure for loneliness," Allison said with a chuckle.

"There you go." She wrapped an arm around her sister-in-law. "Let's go clean up your beautiful kitchen."

Chapter Nine

Tuesday morning dawned cloudy, but still hot and sticky. The weather report called for rain later in the day but the morning was supposed to be dry, which worked out well for Hannah's plan to visit shops and ask about security camera footage from Saturday.

But first, she made coffee. As the rich scent filled her apartment, she fried two eggs and toasted sourdough bread, before sitting with her Bible to read more from 1 Corinthians. Then she quickly got dressed, pulled her hair into a low ponytail, and took out her phone. She scrolled until she found the number for Liam "The Hero" Berthold. She really should delete the nickname, but it amused her.

Your pie is ready. Feel free to stop by the restaurant this afternoon to pick it up.

She worked on the message far longer than she should have, trying to decide whether to add an emoji or make a joke. Finally, she realized she was overthinking and sent it, then held the phone a moment, waiting for the blue dots to appear beneath her message. When they didn't, she told herself she was being ridiculous. She dropped the phone in her bag and headed out the door.

Hannah decided to start at one end of Christine's block and work her way down. The first store, which sat on the corner, was a shop for outdoor enthusiasts. There was a tent set up in the big glass window, with cozy sleeping bags draped over thick air mattresses beside a large cooler and camp stove.

Inside, she walked past a display of hiking poles, boots, and floppy hats, then a section with inflatable kayaks and stand-up paddle boards near the back. Eventually, she found the counter next to a display of ropes and headlamps under a sign that said CAVING.

"Hello." A young man with curly brown hair greeted her enthusiastically. "Can I help you find something?"

"I'm afraid I'm not here to shop," Hannah said. "I'm trying to track down someone who was on this street on Saturday, and I was wondering if the store might have security camera footage that you'd be willing to share."

"We do have a camera outside the shop," he said. "I would have to check with the owner, though, before I could share the footage."

"Of course." Hannah understood. If she had a camera outside the Hot Spot, she wouldn't want her employees giving out the footage to anyone who asked without checking with her.

"Are you with the police?" he asked.

"No," Hannah said. "It's more of a personal matter."

"Okay," he said. "Why don't you leave me your information, and I'll check in with the owner and let you know?"

"That sounds great." She gave him a business card that listed her cell phone number as well as the landline for the Hot Spot. He looked at it and said, "Oh, you own that new restaurant. I hear the burgers are great."

"You should find out for yourself," Hannah said, smiling. "And I do have to admit that the burgers are pretty good, though I might be biased."

"I will," he said. "By the way, we're having a big clearance sale if you want to check out the hiking and camping gear there."

"I think I'm good, but thanks," Hannah said, and waved as she walked to the door.

The next storefront in the row was a copy and printing shop, where the clerk told her they didn't have a camera. Next in line was Seeds of Joy, a store that sold blackberry jam, preserves, and other delicious things made from the town's namesake, as well as products on consignment from local vendors. Hannah talked to owner Shannon Radcliff, who had been friends with her mother. The two updated each other on their lives. Shannon told her they didn't have security cameras, so Hannah moved on to the Thai takeout place, but it wasn't open yet. She didn't see a camera above the door, so she figured she could check that one off her list.

The stationery store beneath Christine's apartment was next, and when Hannah walked in, she was surrounded by boxes of beautiful cards and thick creamy paper. A display of journals took up one part of the wall, with gorgeous wrapping paper on another. It was all beautiful, though Hannah wondered how enough people still sent cards and letters for this place to stay open.

She made her way to the counter, where a girl with big glasses and sandy-blond hair greeted her. "Welcome. Can I help you with something special today?"

"Hi," Hannah said, repeating the now-familiar script. "I'm trying to find someone who was on this street on Saturday, and I was wondering if the store might have security camera footage that you'd be willing to share."

"We do have a camera, but I would need to see if it's okay to share. Can I ask why you want it? I mean, did the person you're searching for do something they shouldn't have?"

"Not necessarily," Hannah said. "But they put something through the mail slot for the apartment above the store, and we're trying to figure out who did it."

"Oh wow." She blinked. "My boss, Carol, owns the whole building, so I imagine she'd be pretty interested in that. But I'll check with her and let you know."

"Thank you," Hannah said. She gave the woman her card and ventured back out to visit a store that sold T-shirts and souvenirs, the dry cleaner, the pizza place, and the pharmacy. At the end, all she had to show for her morning's effort was a handful of people who said they might be able to send her something, maybe.

Well, it was better than nothing. She didn't have any other ideas for how to figure out who had delivered the package to Christine, so she hoped one of those would give her a lead.

She went back to her apartment to change for work and checked her phone. There was a message from Liam.

I can't wait. Is it all right if I stop by around 3 to pick it up?

That would be perfect, Hannah responded.

She finished getting dressed and took an extra moment to make sure her hair was behaving before heading downstairs. As she unlocked the restaurant, her phone rang, and she saw that Lacy was calling.

"Hey," Hannah said, cradling the phone against her ear as she opened the door.

"Hi. I wanted to let you know that I talked to Marshall Fredericks earlier. He's going to do another piece on my egg business. He did one last year, and now he wants to show how it's grown."

"That's wonderful." Marshall had a food blog, *The Gourmet Guy*, and was the food critic for the *Blackberry Valley Chronicle*. He had written a negative review of the Hot Spot when it opened, but his perspective had given Hannah ideas to improve her business. Since then, he'd become a loyal customer. "I'm sure that will be good for business."

"I hope so. Anyway, while he was here, I asked him about the handkerchiefs. You know, because his name starts with *M*."

"What did he say?" She let the door close behind her and flipped on the lights. The hallway flooded with light.

"I think he thought I was crazy."

"So he's not responsible for the packages?"

"Definitely not. Which isn't much of a surprise, seeing as how Marshall can't be older than his midtwenties, but I still had to ask."

"It was worth checking," Hannah agreed.

"I started to read through that stack of letters from Bert, and it's hard to know if there's anything there. He was really into my grandmother—that's clear, at least so far."

"But she married your grandpa."

"Yes, but she saved all Bert's letters. Surely you don't do that if you're uninterested in someone."

"I guess you're right." Hannah walked into the kitchen and turned on the lights in there as well. "Though I imagine at some point she probably forgot she had them. Maybe your grandma's diaries would tell us more. Weren't there dozens of them?"

"You know, you're probably right. If this Bert guy was such a big deal, she probably wrote about him." Then a moment later, Lacy added, "But there are so many of them. Even for the time period his letters cover."

"Maybe we can divide and conquer," Hannah said. "I'll take some."

"Okay," Lacy said. "Maybe Mom can read some too. If we're all reading, it won't feel so daunting. Speaking of Mom, did you get anywhere with the security footage angle?"

"Not yet, but I'm hopeful."

"Keep me posted. I'll let you go. I have to go break up a goat fight."

Hannah laughed as she ended the call. In the kitchen, she washed her hands before she started pulling vegetables from the fridge to begin tonight's dinner prep. It wasn't normally her job, but she was antsy, and routine tasks like slicing vegetables always calmed her.

Her phone rang again as she was chopping ripe tomatoes for the pasta sauce. She didn't recognize the number. After wiping her hands on her apron, she answered the call. "Hello?"

"Hello. Is this Hannah Prentiss?"

"It is," Hannah said.

"Oh, hi, Hannah. This is Carol Hendricks. Are you Gabriel's daughter?"

"I am," Hannah answered. "I moved back to town a few months ago."

"Gabriel and Gordon live on my street. They always make sure to check on me whenever there's a storm. They're such dears. And Gabriel talks about you all the time. He's so proud of you."

"Thank you," Hannah said. She wasn't surprised to hear that her dad and uncle were such good neighbors, but it was gratifying to know nonetheless.

"I own the stationery store. Teegan tells me you were interested in the security camera footage from outside the shop," Carol said. "I wondered if you might tell me why."

"Sure thing. I'm a friend of Christine's daughter, Lacy, and someone slipped something through the mail slot for Christine's apartment. We're trying to figure out who it was."

"Was it something dangerous?" Carol asked with a note of alarm.

"No, not at all," Hannah hurried to assure her. "Something more of a personal nature. She would like to know who delivered it."

"I can understand that," Carol said. "All right. I'll touch base with Christine, to make sure she's on board with this, and then I'll let you know. I may not still have it. I don't know how often it records over itself, but I'll see."

Hannah hung up, uncertain whether she was any closer to getting answers, but it seemed like it could be a step in the right direction. She went back to her tomatoes.

Soon, Jacob arrived, and before long, dinner prep was in full swing. Hannah set a huge pot of water to boil and used a food processor to form a dough that she would make into a tart crust. Once the water was boiling, she slid the peaches in, half a dozen at a time, and then fished them out with a ladle and dunked them in ice water. Then she easily slipped the skins off. Much faster than peeling this many individually. Once all the peaches had been skinned, she sliced them and mixed them with sugar, cinnamon, ginger, and nutmeg. She rolled and shaped the tart crusts then arranged filling neatly on top, popping the first batch into the oven when Elaine appeared in the kitchen.

"Hannah, Liam Berthold is here to see you," she said. "Says you owe him a pie?"

"That's right." Hannah wiped her hands on her apron and took the pie from the industrial refrigerator.

Elaine watched her, one eyebrow raised.

"What?" Hannah wondered if she had something on her face.

"Nothing," Elaine said, a smile spreading over her face. "I mean, half the single women in this town have a crush on Liam Berthold, but he's never shown this much interest in any of them. That's all."

"He's interested in my pie, not in me," Hannah said, rolling her eyes. Why was everyone suddenly so obsessed with her love life? "He helped me with something. I promised him a pie, and he's here to pick it up. That's it."

"Okay," Elaine said, lifting her hands. "It's none of my business anyway."

"I don't have time to date anyone right now."

Elaine grinned again and walked out of the kitchen. Once she stopped scowling after the hostess, Hannah too walked through the swinging doors and into the dining room. Raquel was rolling silverware while Dylan prepped the menus. Liam stood at the entrance, by the hostess stand, in jeans and a T-shirt that hugged his broad shoulders. The sunlight reflected off his black hair, and he beamed at the sight of her. She could see why half the single women in town were interested in Liam, if she was honest. But she didn't have time for things like that.

"There it is," Liam said. "I've been thinking about this pie all day."

"I certainly hope it lives up to your expectations," Hannah said.

"I'm sure it will." As he reached to take it from her, his fingers brushed against hers. "The question is, will it be as good as my grandma's was?"

"Now, that's not fair. Nothing is ever as good as a grandma's food." Hannah had known Liam's grandmother, Miss Bridget, as the librarian in Blackberry Valley. If she was half as good at baking as she was at story time, Hannah didn't have a prayer.

"Perhaps," he said, "But I'm certainly excited to find out."

"You'll have to report back," Hannah said. "Are you taking it to the fire station? Do you need some forks?"

Liam laughed. "That would be really nice of me, wouldn't it? But no, this one's all for me."

Hannah gaped at him. "You're going to eat the whole pie?"

"If it's as good as my grandmother's, I am." He scanned the dining room. "It looks great in here. The memorabilia helps a lot."

"Thank you." Liam had supplied many of the antiques from the fire station and from his own family's personal collection. "I'm happy with how it turned out."

"It smells great too."

"Jacob has a tenderloin cooking."

"Oh man. I'll have to come in for dinner again soon."

"You're welcome anytime." And then, in case he thought she was inviting him specially, she added, "I mean, it's a restaurant, so anyone can come in, but yeah, stop in sometime soon." What was she even saying? Elaine had gotten her all mixed up.

"Sounds good." He smiled at her and walked out.

As she turned away from the door, she saw Elaine at the hostess stand, watching her. Hannah made a point of ignoring her as she walked to the kitchen and got back to work.

When they opened an hour later, the restaurant filled up quickly. Several familiar faces greeted her, and she acknowledged each with a welcoming nod. Dylan took one table's order while Raquel delivered glasses of water to a party in the back. Only one table stood empty, and two couples waited near the front door. They were busier than she'd expected for a Tuesday, but aside from running out of servings of peach tart, things went smoothly. Hannah was kept busy helping Jacob in the kitchen, covering for Elaine when too many people came in at once, and greeting guests to see how they were enjoying their meals.

When they finally closed for the night, she was tired, but happy. The restaurant was still relatively new, and people were still checking it out. And it was summer, when more tourists came through the area to take advantage of the beautiful outdoors around here. But she had several regulars at this point. If they maintained this momentum on weeknights through the fall, they would be in good shape.

It wasn't until she was locking up the restaurant that Hannah saw she'd missed a call from a local number. The call had come in several hours before, at the beginning of the dinner rush. She dialed the number to listen to the voice mail.

"Hi, Hannah, this is Carol from the stationery store again. I got Christine's permission to dig into this, and you're in luck. Teegan helped me find the footage, and it hasn't been recorded over yet. She sent it to the email address on your card. Please let me know if you don't get it or if you need anything else."

Hannah logged into her computer as soon as she returned to her apartment, and sure enough, there was a link to a cloud storage location. When she clicked on it, a black-and-white image appeared on the screen. The camera appeared to be above the door to the stationery shop, but she could see the door to Christine's apartment to the far left.

Hannah pressed play, and the figures on the sidewalk started moving up and down the street. At 8:05 a.m., Deputy Jacky Holt hurried past, clutching a cup of coffee from Jump Start. At 8:07, Connie and Hal Sanchez walked by, hand in hand. It was interesting to see who had been strolling Main Street on Saturday morning, but she quickly realized this was going to take forever.

She sped up the footage to several times the normal speed and focused on Christine's door. That made her task easier, as not many people approached Christine's door. At 10:54, Francine Bagby, the local postal carrier, went by and slid a stack of envelopes into the mail slot. Hannah had already been pretty sure the package hadn't come through the mail, but she could see clearly in the footage that the yellow, padded mailer was not in the stack of mail. Wherever the package had come from, it hadn't been shipped through the US Postal Service.

It was late, and Hannah was starting to think she needed to stop this and get to bed, but then something on the screen caught her eye. At 11:33, someone paused at Christine's door and pushed something through the mail slot.

Hannah's pulse raced. She backed up the footage and watched it again, this time at regular speed.

The woman walked down the street, looking up instead of at the street-level windows on the shops. She wasn't window-shopping. She was looking at the addresses above the doors.

Then, when she spotted the number she was searching for, she smiled, took a now-familiar padded envelope from her bag, and slid it through the mail slot in Christine's door.

But who was she? Hannah watched the footage a third time and paused the video when the woman's face was gazing upward, at the addresses.

Wait. *Hold up.*

Hannah had seen her before.

Chapter Ten

Hannah called Lacy first thing Wednesday morning. As soon as Lacy had finished the farm chores, she raced over to Hannah's apartment to see the security camera footage, a box of her grandmother's leather journals under her arm.

"I grabbed a whole stack of them. Maybe one of them mentions Bert," Lacy said, placing the box on the table.

"I'll go through them later," Hannah promised, pouring her friend a mug of steaming coffee.

They settled at the table, and Hannah opened the file with the footage.

"Here comes Francine," Hannah said, pointing. "You can see her drop off the regular mail through the slot, but you can tell that the padded envelope is not there."

"Right," Lacy agreed. "Which tracks with it not being sent through the mail."

"And then, nearly an hour later, watch this." She advanced the footage until the woman came into view. "See how she's looking above the doors?"

"She's reading the addresses," Lacy said, and Hannah nodded.

"And then, you can see her spot the right number." Hannah let the film play and Lacy gasped as, onscreen, the woman pulled a yellow, padded envelope out of her bag and slipped it through the mail slot.

"Wow. That's her." Lacy clapped her hands. "I suppose it's safe to assume she's the same one who delivered the envelope to my place?"

"I guess we can't know at this point, but I would say that's a fair assumption for now anyway. At minimum, we know she's involved somehow."

Lacy sipped her coffee. "Now, who is she? I've never seen her before, and I have no idea who she is or why she delivered the envelopes."

"That's the thing," Hannah said. "I recognize her."

Eyes widening in surprise, Lacy asked, "What? How?"

"I met her," Hannah said. "I don't know her, or how to find her again. But she came into the restaurant Saturday night. I only talked to her briefly, but she told me her name was Madison."

Lacy gasped. "*M.*"

"Exactly."

"So how do we talk to her?"

Hannah hadn't quite figured this part out yet. "I don't know, to be honest. I've been racking my brain, and that's literally all I can remember about her. I don't have a clue how to track her down."

"Okay. Do we know who else might know more about her?"

"I figured I would ask Raquel if she learned anything about her. Raquel waited on her when she ate at the restaurant."

"It's a good start." Lacy leaned forward and paused the footage where Madison's face was most visible. "She doesn't look like anyone

I know. I guess I was hoping that if I saw her face directly, it would be clear who she was. Maybe a long-lost relative."

"I guess it would be nice to find out you had more family than you thought, even if it led to a bunch of questions."

"I agree, but honestly, this girl doesn't look like she's related to me at all."

Hannah looked from Lacy's reddish-brown hair and hazel eyes to the girl's light hair and eyes. A relative seemed unlikely, but it wasn't out of the question. "Genetics can be funny, so I would hesitate to rule out the possibility based on hair or eye color, but I do think we shouldn't go too far down that road without talking to your mom."

Hannah thought for a moment. "But what if the connection doesn't involve your mom? What if it goes back farther than that?"

"You're thinking about Bert Meisel again?"

"I am," Hannah said.

"I finished his letters last night," Lacy said. "They were pretty interesting."

"What did they say?"

"Well, it was a little challenging to piece their story together. I only had the letters he wrote to Grandma, so it was like hearing one side of a conversation, but I got the gist. It sounds like he met her at a church picnic when she was in high school. He had been in the area to visit his cousin, and it sounds like he swept her off her feet."

"That's sweet."

"Well, yes, except that she was kind of seeing my grandpa at the time."

"Whoops."

"She ended it with Grandpa for a while. Bert tells her about college and what Boston is like, and how he can't wait to show it to her. It would have been hard for a girl from a small mining town to not fall for him. He was showing her a world so unlike the one she lived in. A chance at a better life—or at least the kind she could only imagine."

"So what happened?"

"The letters became less and less frequent, and then the last one says he found someone else, and he wasn't going to write to Grandma any longer."

Hannah gasped. "How could he do that to her?"

"I don't know how she took it. Not well, I'm sure, but that was the last letter she got from him. She must have gotten back together with Grandpa, because she married him a few years later."

Hannah wished Helen were still around so they could ask her more about what had happened. To say nothing of her husband, Walter. Had he secretly felt like a consolation prize after being dumped for the big-city boy, until Bert lost interest? Then again, it wasn't any of Hannah's business. She only needed to know how Bert fit into this mystery—if at all.

"Is there any indication they saw each other after that first church picnic?" Hannah asked.

"No," Lacy said. "And since Mom wasn't born until a year after Grandma married Grandpa, I don't think there's any sordid secret here."

"I'm glad for that, but it's frustrating that this hasn't led us anywhere."

"I don't think Bert is likely to have much to do with this, sadly."

"Oh well." Hannah sighed. "I'll ask Raquel if she learned anything about Madison while she was waiting on her. And I haven't heard back from any of the other people I asked about security camera footage. Maybe one of them has a recording that might tell us more about her. Meanwhile, I guess you could ask your mom about any distant relatives."

"I'm sure that will go smoothly. I'm not sure I need any more tense conversations with her right now."

Hannah recalled the conversation she'd had with Christine at her apartment. Perhaps it wasn't her place, but if she could help smooth out the tension between mother and daughter, she wouldn't pass up the chance. "At the risk of sticking my nose where it doesn't belong—when I was talking to your mom the other day, I got the impression she wanted to move back to the farm. It sounded like she thought she would be intruding, not that she didn't want to be there."

Lacy gaped at her. "She wouldn't be intruding."

"I'm not sure she knows that. I'm sure you've told her otherwise, but she might have thought you were merely being polite, rather than that you very much want her there."

"Really?"

"It was an impression I got. Maybe it's not accurate." Hannah was pretty sure it was, though. "Anyway, it sounds like you have enough to do, and I'll ask Raquel when she comes in if she remembers anything about this Madison person. We'll find her somehow."

It took every ounce of Hannah's self-control not to pounce on Raquel the moment she came into the restaurant. She waited until the young woman was absorbed in updating the specials on a big chalkboard on the wall before she walked up and asked her if she remembered a customer from Saturday night.

"Which one?"

"She was a young blond woman who sat by herself. She said her name was Madison."

"Oh yeah. I remember her. She was nice. She ordered the Inferno Wings, and then she had the Five Alarm Burger, as well as dessert. I wondered where she was able to put it all because she was so skinny."

"Did you talk with her at all?"

"Sure. I asked her where she was visiting from. She told me she'd recently graduated from the University of Kentucky and was living at home with her parents while she figures out what she wants to do next."

"Did she tell you where she's living? Or anything about her parents?"

"I don't think so." Raquel considered for a moment. "She said she'd been to Jump Start Coffee and Legend & Key. She talked about how every place she'd visited in town had been like something out of a novel. She did appear to like books. She was reading one while she ate. I noticed that because most people who eat alone stare at their phones, but she had a book, which I thought was cool."

"Do you know what book it was?"

"*The Count of Monte Cristo*. She said she'd read it before, but she liked it because it was a tale of patient revenge."

Hannah raised her eyebrows. "That's an intense take."

"I know, right?" Raquel replied. "I've never read it, but it was a big, thick book."

Hannah had read it years before. It was good, but huge. And it was a tale of revenge, played out over most of a lifetime. Did that resonate with Madison for a particular reason? Could the envelopes have to do with revenge?

"Did she say anything about what brought her to town?"

Raquel frowned. "I don't think so. I'm sorry. Should I have asked her?"

"No. It would have been weird to grill her too much."

"I would happily have done so, if I'd known you wanted to know."

"I would have done it myself if I'd known," Hannah assured her.

"Why? What's this all about?"

"We're trying to track her down because she hand-delivered an envelope to Christine's apartment." Hannah realized Raquel was staring at her in open confusion. "It's... complicated."

"Okay. Well, if I remember anything else about her, I'll let you know." Raquel picked up the chalk again then paused. "You know, I've been meaning to mention something. I have this cousin, Victor, and he's a great guy. Good job, sweetest thing ever, and he can't find the right woman. I was thinking you guys would get along."

Hannah took a deep breath. Raquel was trying to be kind. Hannah wouldn't point out that Raquel herself was single, so perhaps she should find someone for herself before worrying about Hannah. "You're great to think of me, but I'm not interested in dating anyone right now."

"You sure? Victor's super cute."

"I'm sure he is. If anything changes, I'll let you know. But right now I'm focusing on the restaurant."

Raquel shrugged. "All right."

"Thank you for thinking of me, though." As frustrating as it was to have people continually trying to set her up, Hannah knew that it came from a good place. She wouldn't let it get to her. She wasn't the only thirtysomething in this town who hadn't gotten married right out of high school. It wasn't *that* strange to be single at her age, right?

Hannah walked away and tried to focus on what she'd learned about Madison, not Raquel's cousin. She knew Madison had recently graduated from the University of Kentucky. She knew she had been reading a classic tale of revenge that was hundreds of pages long. That suggested she liked books. And revenge? Or maybe just books. All of which was more than Hannah had known before.

She knew Madison could put away a lot of food despite her tiny size. Not that that would help Hannah find her. But the university thing was something to go on. There had to be a way to figure out how to contact recent graduates of the university. Maybe Hannah could contact the UK alumni association or something. She would dig into that as soon as she had a chance. For now, she had a restaurant to open in an hour, and there was still a lot to do.

But halfway through dinner service, she had an idea.

Chapter Eleven

Hannah was at the library as soon as it opened Thursday morning.

"Our first customer." Evangeline Cooke, the head librarian, held open the door for Hannah. "Come on in. It's going to be a hot one, isn't it?" Evangeline was in her sixties and wore her long silvery hair in a messy bun above an ever-present smile.

"It sure is," Hannah said as a wave of cool air hit her. "It feels heavenly in here, though."

"As it should. Books are a welcome retreat," Evangeline said. "Is there anything I can help you with?"

Hannah hesitated. She had no idea if her idea was a good one or not. "I'm trying to find out about someone who recently graduated from the University of Kentucky. Is there a database or something I could search?" Hannah's mom had loved books and had taught Hannah that she could find the answer to any question at the library.

"I'm sure there's an alumni directory, but I imagine you would need to be an alumnus to be able to search it. Did she go to high school in the area, by chance?"

"I don't think so," Hannah said.

"Too bad. As you know, we have most of the yearbooks in the local history room."

Hannah had used the yearbooks not long ago to solve a mystery, and they were a treasure trove of information about Blackberry Valley.

Evangeline pressed her lips together then said, "I could call my friend who works at the library in Lexington. It's possible they have resources there. I can see what I can find out. What do you want to know?"

"Her last name, and ideally, how to get in touch with her," Hannah said. "And why she was in Blackberry Valley on Saturday, though I doubt your friend will be able to tell me that."

"Okay. It's a bit harder without a last name, but that will make for a fun puzzle. What's her first name?"

"Madison."

"Do you know anything else about her?"

"She's blond. She says she just graduated, so I'm assuming that means this year. She likes to read, so maybe she majored in English?"

"That's not a lot to go on, but I'll see what my friend can find."

"Thank you so much."

"Can I help you with anything else in the meantime?"

Hannah had a second item on her list of things to research. "I'm also trying to find information on someone else. I have a last name this time."

"That's always a good thing."

"I think he would be quite old if he's still alive." Hannah knew the chance of Bert Meisel being involved with the mystery packages was slim, but figured it was worth seeing what she could find out about him anyway.

"I would start with a newspaper search, if it were me," Evangeline said. "You could search for marriage announcements, an obituary, that sort of thing."

"That's a good idea."

"Let's get you set up at one of the computers." Evangeline led her to the first computer in a long row and opened a program. "The newspaper database is right here." The librarian showed her how to adjust the search parameters, to filter for location and time frame, and to search by keyword.

Once Evangeline returned to work, Hannah typed in the name *Bert Meisel* and hit return. It took a few tries, but eventually, she found an obituary for Gilbert Meisel from Louisville, Kentucky. She read it quickly. Gilbert had been born—and graduated from high school—in Louisville before going off to Harvard to study engineering. He married Elizabeth Jane Dougal in March of 1958 in her hometown of Andover, Massachusetts, and they had three children together. Their children and grandchildren were listed, but the names weren't familiar to Hannah. There was no connection to Christine or Lacy as far as Hannah could see. It was time to cross Bert off her list.

But that left few names *on* the list. Lacy and Christine didn't think it could be Marilyn, Christine's godmother. But Hannah might as well do a little research while she was at the library. Helen's friend might not have anything to do with the mystery packages, but it couldn't hurt to see what she could learn. She typed in the name and hit return again.

The first thing that came up was Marilyn's obituary in the *Harlan County Times,* which appeared to be a weekly newspaper in eastern Kentucky. She had passed away after a long battle with cancer, survived by her husband, two daughters, three sons, and twelve grandchildren. None were named Madison.

Hannah poked around in the newspaper archive a bit more but couldn't find anything else about Marilyn. That was a shame, but unless there was some connection to Madison, she didn't see how Marilyn could be connected anyway.

Finally, she turned to the last item on her list, taking out the photo of the poem she'd taken and the notes she'd made when she'd seen it again in person. Then she flipped to a fresh page in her notebook. She copied out the poem as well as she could.

Long years... cannot fill—
The absence...
Embers of a thousand years
They were fire
And understand—

Hannah clicked around on the computer, searching for some kind of poetry database or anything else she could compare the piece to, but didn't find anything. She was sure she could find books of poetry on the shelves, but she would be choosing volumes at random and flipping through, hoping to find anything that might match. That didn't seem like the best approach.

She glanced at the circulation desk. If anyone could make sense of a fragment of poetry, it would be a librarian, and Evangeline didn't appear busy.

"Any luck?" Evangeline asked as Hannah approached the desk.

"I'm not sure yet."

"Well, that's better than a no." Evangeline giggled. "I spoke with my friend in Lexington, and she thinks they have a recent yearbook from the college on hand. She's going to let me know when she finds it."

"Thank you so much. Now I have another strange question."

"My favorite kind. What do you need?"

"I have what I think is a fragment of a poem," Hannah said. "I don't know what it's from or what it means, and I'm not quite sure where to start searching."

"Can I see?"

Hannah slid the notebook paper across the desk.

Evangeline looked down, her brow furrowing. "This dash here," she said, tapping on the dash at the end of the first line. "Does it show up in the poem like that?"

"Yes," Hannah said. "The one after 'understand' too. Here's the original." She pulled up the photo she'd taken on her phone.

Glancing at the screen, Evangeline touched a finger to her chin. "I don't know for sure, but that looks like Emily Dickinson to me."

"It does?"

"Short lines ending in dashes is very typical of her style," Evangeline said. "I don't recognize the poem itself, but..." She turned to the computer on her desk and typed on her keyboard for a moment. "Here it is. Poem '1383,'" Evangeline said with a smile.

"Wait. What?" Hannah leaned forward to see the screen better. "Did you use a plain old search engine to solve this?"

Evangeline chuckled. "I suppose if you'd prefer, I could go get the volume of Emily Dickinson's poetry and read through every poem, but there are 1800 of them. It would take forever. This was much quicker."

"I should have tried that. It didn't even occur to me. And you knew it was Emily Dickinson because of the dash?" Hannah should have paid more attention in English class.

"It's very much her style. Come on. I'll show you." She led Hannah into the stacks and stopped in the poetry section, where she withdrew a thick volume from the shelf. She flipped through the pages, and Hannah saw that each page showed a short poem surrounded by plenty of white space. Many of the lines ended with a dash. "Here we are. '1383,' likely written around 1876."

> Long Years apart — can make no
> Breach a second cannot fill —
> The absence of the Witch does not
> Invalidate the spell —
> The embers of a Thousand Years
> Uncovered by the Hand
> That fondled them when they were Fire
> Will stir and understand —

Hannah read the words. Then she read them again, trying to make sense of them. "Is that the whole poem?"

"It is."

"With the dash at the end, it almost seems as if there's more coming."

"That's fairly typical of Dickinson's poetry."

"It's about friendship, and how long separation doesn't make a difference?" Hannah ventured.

"That's precisely how I read it."

"What's that bit about fire, though?"

Evangeline looked at the page again. "I think it means that even something that hurt a relationship—'fondled them when they were fire'—doesn't make it any less real or true."

"So, it's about missing someone you've hurt and been apart from?"

"That's one way to read it. It's poetry. There are a thousand ways to read it."

Hannah read the poem again, trying to understand. Was the person behind the packages a long-lost friend? Someone Christine hadn't seen in a long time because of a past hurt? Was this their way of asking forgiveness? But if so, why not say who it was from? And what was with the key and the handkerchief? And what about the package for Lacy? Hers didn't have the poem, but it had clearly been delivered by the same person.

"You seem even more confused now than you were before," Evangeline observed.

"I'm sorry. Thank you for all you've done. I'm sure it will help, knowing what the poem is."

"What's the story with the poem, if you don't mind my asking?"

"You know my friend, Lacy Minyard?" When Evangeline nodded, Hannah told her about the packages.

"That's very strange," Evangeline said. "Does she have any long-lost friends?"

"Not that I know of. I'll have to ask."

"Well, you know at least one thing—whoever sent it seems to like Emily Dickinson's poetry."

"That's not much to go on."

"It's not nothing though." Evangeline smiled. "Maybe it would help to learn more about Emily Dickinson. Maybe something about her is the key here."

"Didn't Emily Dickinson live in a garret in New England and, like, never see anyone?" That was pretty much the extent of Hannah's knowledge about the poet.

"That's not exactly true," Evangeline said. "She never married, and she was something of a recluse in New England. But there's a whole lot more to her than that. We have a great biography about her. Would you like me to go get it for you?"

"Sure." Hannah didn't see how it would help, but she couldn't rule out the possibility.

Evangeline retrieved the biography and Hannah checked it out, along with the volume of Dickinson's poetry. She had a bit of time before she needed to head in to the restaurant, so she decided to tackle the next item on her list.

Raquel had mentioned that Madison visited several businesses while she'd been in town. Perhaps Madison had spoken to someone at one of those places, unintentionally leaving behind another clue. Hannah decided to head to Jump Start first. The coffee shop smelled delicious when she walked inside. She walked up to the register and greeted Zane.

"Hi, Hannah," he replied. "What can I get you today?"

"I'll take an iced coffee, please," Hannah said. "And I have an odd question."

"Shoot." Zane filled a plastic cup with ice.

"I'm trying to find a young woman who was in town on Saturday, and I believe she came in here. I was wondering if you might have spoken to her."

"Can you describe her? A lot of people come in here, especially on weekends."

"She's young—probably early twenties. Blond hair. She was wearing a tennis-style skirt," Hannah said. "I think she would have been alone, most likely."

"That does sound kind of familiar. She was perky, from out of town?"

"Exactly," Hannah said.

"If we're thinking of the same person, she went on and on about how cute the town is, but that was the extent of our conversation. Oh, except that she ordered a blended mocha, which takes a bit to make, especially during a rush like that. That's all I remember."

Hannah had loved those sweet drinks when she was young too. Now it was harder to justify drinking what amounted to a milkshake when she wanted coffee. "If you think of anything else, will you let me know?"

"Sure."

Hannah wasn't optimistic about further information from Zane, but she was hopeful that she might learn something at Legend & Key.

Neil smiled when she walked into the bookstore, coffee in hand. "Hey there, Hannah."

"I'll have you know that I don't intend to spend any money here today."

Neil laughed. "That wasn't why I was glad to see you. Though for the record, you are one of our best customers."

"And my bank account knows it," she said. "I'm chasing a lead on those envelopes. Did Lacy tell you we have video of the woman who dropped them off?"

"Yep," he said. "That's pretty crazy, isn't it?"

"Apparently she came in here at some point on Saturday."

"She did? Did she buy anything?"

"I don't know."

"I always remember customers by what they buy."

"I do know that she was reading *The Count of Monte Cristo* at the Hot Spot that evening, but I don't know if she bought it here."

"Nope. Haven't sold any of those recently." Neil shook his head. "Lacy said the mystery woman was young and blond?"

"That's right. She was wearing a skirt."

"Doesn't ring a bell," Neil said. "I'll have to think about it some more. We had so many people in on Saturday. I wonder if she knew about my connection to Lacy, or whether it was mere chance that she came in here."

"It sounds like she visited a few places in town," Hannah said. "It seems she was enjoying her time here."

"I'm curious about her. Please let me know what you find out," Neil said. "And I'm still working on that mountain thing, by the way. I know I've seen that symbol before. I just need to figure out where."

"If you think of it, please let me know," Hannah said. Neil promised he would, and she returned to her apartment to finish her coffee and drop off the library books before heading to the restaurant.

Amos Bowers was scheduled to deliver the restaurant's first order of grass-fed beef, and Lacy would also drop off more eggs after the lunch rush.

But she still had a few minutes before she needed to head to the restaurant. Hannah eyed the box of journals Lacy had brought over. She picked up the top one and opened it. *Helen Frances Whitmore, 1950* was recorded on the first page. Helen would have been twelve. There wouldn't be any mentions of Bert, since she hadn't met him yet, but it would be nice to learn a bit more about what Helen was like when she was younger.

> *January 1, 1950*
>
> *Dad says this year is going to be a good one. He thinks the war is going to end soon and Uncle Gerry will come home. In the meantime, there's plenty of work in the mines, so we're lucky.*
>
> *I guess he means it, though it doesn't seem like such a good one so far. It's cold and rainy here, and when I go back to school in a few days, I have to recite a poem. I've spent some time every day making sure I have it committed to memory. Josie Nye says she wouldn't waste time off doing schoolwork, so it will be interesting to see what happens when it's her turn to recite. Marilyn has been working on hers, but it takes her a long time.*
>
> *I've decided I'm going to save up enough money to buy a bicycle this year, and I started to put aside the money I earn from collecting rags. It will be a sacrifice, but it will be worth it. I hope.*

January 2, 1950

The whole house still smells like boiled cabbage. Mom says we're lucky to be able to afford corned beef for New Year's dinner, but I don't think it's so lucky to have to eat something that feels like stringy leather.

I made good progress on the blanket I'm knitting for Francesca Pierson's—now Dalton's—baby. I'm using yellow yarn. Nancy says I should have used pink, because she's certain it's going to be a girl, but that's not prudent. Just wanting it doesn't make it so, and this way it works no matter what. Nancy can make her own blanket if she wants to use pink. Marilyn says her sister will love it either way.

Nancy has spent most of the break reading the stack of books she got from the library, which has been nice because it means she's not bothering me.

January 3, 1950

Back to school today, and I managed to get through my poem with only a couple of mistakes. Josie laughed, but then she messed up on her own poem so there.

The journal entries continued in the same vein for nearly every day of the year, with Helen recounting the daily trials and highlights of a young girl's life. A picture of Helen as a studious, dedicated, and practical girl emerged. Hannah was intrigued by the mention of the poems, but as she read more, she saw that there was no detail regarding which poem Helen had memorized, so there was no way to know if it was connected to the poem that had come in the package.

However, throughout the year, Marilyn, who had become Christine's godmother, showed up frequently, and she appeared to be a kind, good friend to Helen.

Hannah was also intrigued by the mention of Nancy, the sister Helen had fallen out of touch with at some point. Nancy seemed to be more free-spirited than Helen, but pretty much anyone would come across as more free-spirited than Helen, based on what Hannah was reading. The anecdotes in the journal struck her as typical sister stuff. What had happened between the two to sever their relationship permanently? She hoped one of the other journals might offer some clue.

She skimmed most of the entries for references to Nancy or Marilyn, but there weren't as many as she might have hoped. When she got to the end of the first journal, she set it aside and opened the next one in the stack. This one was from 1960, when Helen was married and had young Christine. The family still lived in Russell at the time, before the move to Lexington. The entries revealed the trudge of life with a young child, the endless diapers and naps and sleepless nights. Helen adored her baby, that was clear, but also found it draining to be alone with her all day while her husband was at work in the mines.

There were more mentions of Nancy throughout, so whatever had happened between the sisters didn't come until later. No additional comment on the poems, though, or anything about handkerchiefs or keys. Nobody suspicious with an *M* name. She closed the journal and eyed the stack. There were a lot of years left, and the entries, as informative as they might be, became a bit tedious after a while.

Hannah set aside the journal. She needed to get going if they were going to open the restaurant on time. She got ready for work and hurried downstairs.

When Lacy arrived with the order of eggs, Hannah told her what she'd learned at the library.

"Emily Dickinson?" Lacy said, furrowing her brow. "I mean, that's great, and thank you for finding the poem. But who would send Mom an Emily Dickinson poem?"

"Can you ask her if she knows anyone with a fondness for Emily Dickinson?"

"Sure. Maybe it will be a super-obvious message once she knows what it's supposed to say." But Lacy looked as dubious as Hannah felt.

Hannah also updated her about the search for Madison and what she'd learned about Bert and Marilyn.

"Yeah, those were always a stretch, so I think we should drop that line of questioning for good," Lacy said. "But please let me know if Evangeline is able to find out more about Madison."

Hannah promised she would, and when Lacy left, Hannah continued getting the restaurant ready to open for dinner.

They were only about half an hour from opening when Hannah got a call from Evangeline.

"Hello?" Hannah said, pressing her finger to her other ear to hear over the noise of Dylan setting down the chairs in the dining room.

"I found her," Evangeline said, her voice breathless with excitement. "That girl you were looking for—Madison? I know who she is."

Chapter Twelve

H er name is Madison Maris," Evangeline said.

Madison Maris. Her name had not one *M*, but two!

"She graduated this past May, according to the yearbook my friend found. She was an English major from Harlan, Kentucky. She was on the volleyball team and sang in an a cappella group called The Treble Tones."

"Wow." Hannah grabbed a napkin and jotted it all down. "That's great. You're sure it's her?"

"She's the only person named Madison with blond hair in the senior class, though people can color their hair. I'll text you the photo my friend sent me so you can make sure."

"That would be amazing. Thank you so much."

"My pleasure. Let me know if you have any more puzzles to solve. It's way more exciting than reshelving picture books."

"I absolutely will."

A moment after Hannah hung up, a text came through with a photo of the now-familiar Madison. It was her, all right.

Now that Hannah had a last name, it couldn't be that hard to find her. Hannah didn't have time to start researching her now, but as soon as she had a moment, she would see what she could figure out.

But for now, she had a more immediate problem. When Elaine unlocked the doors to open the restaurant for dinner, the first person who walked in was Mitch Thomas.

Hannah ducked into the kitchen. "How's it going in here?"

"About the same as it was two minutes ago when you left." Jacob was scraping off the grill. "Everything is under control."

"Do you need any help?"

"We don't have any orders yet," Jacob reminded her drily. "So for now, I think we've got it."

"I'll take a peek at the crumble." The peach tarts had been a big hit last night, but since blackberries were the specialty, she'd made blackberry crumble with vanilla whipped cream. Usually Jacob handled dessert, but sometimes she got inspired and jumped in, and the bushels of ripe blackberries that had been delivered today had made her crave crumble. Sure enough, everything looked good.

She couldn't hide all night. She forced herself to step out into the dining room. Mitch sat alone at a table by the window, and he looked up when he saw Hannah. She should go over and talk to him. It would be too obvious if she didn't.

"Hi, Mitch," she said, walking up to the table. "Thanks for coming in."

"You're a hard woman to track down," he said, a big grin on his face. "I was hoping to talk to you after church on Sunday, but you had too many suitors."

"I don't have any suitors." She tried not to make it sound defensive.

"Trust me—I understand why you'd be talking to Ryder and Liam."

This conversation had already taken a weird turn. "Ryder is my cousin. I promise he wasn't trying to ask me out."

"Well, anyway, I figured that if I wanted a shot, I needed to be bold, so here I am."

"Here you are." She didn't know what else to say.

"It's a great space," he said. "And I've heard amazing things about the food."

"If you like hamburgers, you should try the Rookie Meltdown," Hannah said. "It's one of our bestsellers. But the pork and chicken are great too."

"Do you see yourself running a restaurant long-term?" Mitch cocked his head.

What? Did anyone start a restaurant without the hope that it would last for the long term? "I hope so. My goal is to make the business profitable enough that I can keep the doors open. It's always been my dream to have my own restaurant," she added.

"Even when you have kids?"

"I don't see why I couldn't do both," Hannah said. Was he grilling her about her future plans? Was this some kind of test? "But kids are so far in my future that I'm not really concerned about that yet."

"But you *do* want kids," he said, and it was clear what the right answer should be.

"I always figured I would have some someday."

He lifted his chin. "That's good. My first wife didn't want kids. That's a big part of why we divorced."

It was officially time to get out of this conversation. "If you'll excuse me, I have to go check something in the kitchen." She fled through the swinging doors, ignoring the knowing grin Elaine flashed her.

"Still under control," Jacob said.

"I know. I need to hide out here for a while," Hannah said. "I'm going to work on my new recipe for Kentucky Hot Browns."

"Right now?"

"Yes." Though she could see why he had said it like that. Dinner service would soon be in full swing. If she started messing around with a new recipe, getting in the way and using up ingredients he'd already prepped for the meals on the menu, it would make things much more difficult for him. She knew better than to start testing recipes in the middle of dinner service. What was she thinking? "You're right," she said. "I won't do it now."

"I do want to try your idea, but maybe another time," Jacob said.

Hannah opened the walk-in fridge. It was immaculate, as usual. Jacob kept it clean, and Hannah double-checked it as often as possible. It felt nice and cool, and she took a moment to be grateful that she didn't have a massive bill to repair the new fridge.

However, perhaps there was a better way to organize the contents. Maybe she should separate these ingredients by category, and then arrange them by alphabetical order within each category, with the oldest items at the front. And those bins of peppers, kale, and yellow squash would be prettier in baskets. Hannah got to work, being sure to examine each piece of food as she picked it up, though she knew everything would be fine.

She stepped out in time to overhear Jacob saying in a puzzled tone, "...she decided it was a good time to clean the fridge."

Raquel stood in the open doorway. Her arms were crossed over her chest, and she had an eyebrow raised. "Table Seven would like to see you."

That was Mitch. "Why? Is everything all right?"

"I don't know. He asked if you were around, and I said I would see if you were available."

"As you can see, I'm not, so—"

Raquel interrupted. "So you want me to tell the perfectly nice man who has come in here to see you, and who has not yet cashed out his bill or calculated his tip, that you're too busy cleaning out the walk-in fridge to talk to him?"

Well, when she said it that way, Hannah could see how it would put Raquel in an awkward position.

"Okay," Hannah said, resigned. "I'm coming." She opened a container of tomato sauce, sniffed it, and then tossed it for good measure before she followed Raquel out to the dining room.

Mitch smiled as she approached his table. "It must be a busy night. You're working so hard."

"There's always work to do with a restaurant," Hannah said.

"Yes, well, the food was excellent," Mitch said. "But what I came here for was to ask if you'd go out to dinner with me. Not here. I mean, if you wanted to eat here, that would be fine, but I figured you'd want to go somewhere else. Or we don't have to eat, if you'd rather see a movie or something."

It was the moment she'd been dreading. For a second, she considered agreeing to avoid having an awkward conversation in her place of business. It would be easier to delay it. But she knew she would spend every minute leading up to their date dreading it, and the longer she delayed the rejection, the harder it would be to give. Liam had been right. Instead of avoiding Mitch, it would have been kinder to be up-front about how she felt.

"That's very kind of you, Mitch," she said. "I bet you're a great guy." It was true—he did seem to be kind and thoughtful. He knew what he wanted in a long-term relationship, based on the questions he'd asked her earlier. But unfortunately, what he was searching for wasn't her. "But I'm afraid I'm not interested in dating anyone at the moment. The restaurant takes so much time and work. It wouldn't be fair of me to start a dating relationship right now. But thank you for asking."

"I see." He took in a deep breath and let it out slowly. "Well, thank you for being honest. It wasn't what I wanted to hear, but so many times, women don't say what they really want. I appreciate you saving us both the frustration."

It wasn't the most romantic speech, but Hannah was grateful that he was taking it so well. It was maybe a bit clinical, but she understood that he was saying what they both knew. There was no point in pretending she was interested in him to save his feelings, and hiding from him instead of being honest was childish—she could see that now—so even though this wasn't her favorite conversation ever, she was glad she'd been direct.

Hannah thanked him again for coming to the Hot Spot, and then she walked over to Raquel and asked her to bring him a dessert on the house.

That was one problem solved. Now if only she could find an answer to the rest of them.

Chapter Thirteen

Before she went to bed Thursday night, Hannah reread the Emily Dickinson poem, hoping to spot a connection to the keys or the handkerchiefs. There was no mountain mentioned, and nothing that could be interpreted as a reference to a key. Emily Dickinson didn't start with an *M*. Though it did start with an *Em*. It seemed like a stretch that that might mean anything.

Madison had been an English major, according to Evangeline. Was she the Dickinson fan? But why that poem, and what did it have to do with anything?

Frustrated, Hannah read a few of the other poems in the collection. There were a lot of them, for sure, but there were a few she recognized.

"Hope" is a thing with feathers—

Because I could not stop for Death—
He kindly stopped for me—

Tell all the truth but tell it slant—

She set the poetry book aside and picked up the biography of Emily Dickinson. It was well-written, which made for an entertaining read.

Emily was from a wealthy family in Massachusetts. Her grandfather had helped start Amherst College, and her father had been a lawyer and served a term in Congress. She had a brother and a sister she was close to. Emily and her sister, Lavinia, never married, while her brother, Austin, married and lived next door.

Emily was something of a recluse, at some points refusing to come out of her room to greet visitors. She would talk to them through the door, when she would talk to them at all. Only ten of her nearly 1,800 poems were published in her lifetime. She was now considered to be one of the most important American poets of the nineteenth century.

Which was all very interesting, but Hannah didn't see what it had to do with the mystery she was trying to solve.

She gave up and went to bed, dreaming of garrets and fire and endless manuscript pages of scrawled words she couldn't make out.

Hannah woke up bleary-eyed on Friday, but with renewed determination. The sky was gray and the clouds hung low and heavy, matching her mood. She didn't know what Emily Dickinson had to do with the envelopes Lacy and Christine had received, but she did know that Madison was involved. Hannah intended to spend the morning figuring out how.

But first, coffee.

After she'd finished her second cup and her Bible reading for the day, Hannah opened her laptop and clicked on a new browser window. First, she tried a simple search for the name *Madison Maris*.

A social media page came up first, displaying dozens of video reviews Madison had filmed about books she enjoyed. Hannah clicked on one and watched Madison rapturously describing the plot of a romance book she'd read. It didn't sound like Hannah's taste—too angsty, and without enough plot—but she had to appreciate anyone who used social media to talk about books.

The next video was about a different book, but was basically the same, with Madison gushing about the characters and their romance and how much she'd loved it, though this story apparently involved dragons. It didn't take long to discover that all her videos were pretty similar. The comments sections held dozens of remarks, and they mostly said things that equated to *I can't wait to read this book*, but with a lot of emojis. Madison had quite the following. Hannah didn't know a ton about these things, but the number of followers listed seemed high to her.

She played another video and studied the background. Madison appeared to be in a bedroom. The room behind her was neat and mostly in shadow, and as much as Hannah tried, she couldn't make out anything that would tell her about where it was filmed.

The same background appeared in the most recent eight or so videos, but the ones filmed before then were in a different room, this one smaller and brighter. Still nothing that would tell her where Madison was, though Hannah guessed she had been in college when these were filmed.

Hannah thought she could send Madison a message through the platform. Poking around, she tried to figure out how to do that, only to discover that she would have to create an account of her own. She never used this platform and didn't particularly want to give her information. In any case, Madison's account appeared to be full of videos that wouldn't tell Hannah much, but she would come back to the site if she got desperate. She decided to move on to see what else she could find.

She returned to the main search page and found links to a different social media site, one that was mostly image-based. Most of the same videos had been posted on this platform too, but Madison had fewer followers here. Mixed in with the videos were selfies of Madison with flattering camera angles and good lighting.

Hannah clicked on a photo of Madison posing with several other young women in cute dresses, their arms around one another. Underneath the photo it said *#springfling #senioryear #whoneedsdates*. The other women had been tagged as well. Clicking on the handle for one of them, Hannah saw that it was the girl with curly dark hair on the left. Her name was Nena, and her feed was filled with selfies. Another girl who had been tagged was named Esther, and her feed consisted mostly of artistic photos of sunsets, coffee mugs, and journals and pens. If there was a clue to be found in the social media accounts of Madison's friends, Hannah didn't know what it was.

She clicked to the main search page and found several links to articles in the college newspaper that mentioned Madison. She'd apparently been very good at volleyball and had made a few game-winning plays that gained mention in the sports section. She'd also been interviewed as part of a feature where the paper had asked seniors about their plans after graduation.

"I'm still trying to figure out what I want to do," says Madison Maris. "For now, I'm headed home to eastern Kentucky, the prettiest place in the world. After that, my dream is to go to New York. I'd love to work in book publishing."

Surely she would have mentioned it in one of her videos if she had moved to New York and was working in book publishing. It was more likely Madison was still in eastern Kentucky. But what had she been doing in Blackberry Valley on Saturday?

Whatever the answers were, Hannah wasn't finding them here. And while she was glad to know Madison's last name, she still hadn't figured out a good way to get in touch with her.

She kept scrolling through the pages, looking for something useful, and was about to give up when her phone rang with a call from Lacy.

Hannah scooped it up. "Good morning."

"Neil remembered where he's seen the mountain image before."

"What?"

"The image on the key? It's been driving him crazy, but he couldn't remember where he'd seen it. He was going through books and searching online, and this morning, he was poking around in some old plat maps to see our property line and how the farm had grown over time, and he remembered where he'd seen it before."

"Why was he looking at how your farm grew over time?"

"He had an idea that maybe the key unlocked something that didn't used to be on our property but is now. Which is not a bad idea, although he didn't find much. But sorting through the maps did knock something loose in his brain, and now he's saying you should meet him at the library in twenty minutes."

"I'll be there," Hannah said.

Hannah found herself standing outside the library doors when Evangeline unlocked them once again.

"Hey there. Two days in a row?" the librarian said, pushing the door open.

"I can't get enough," Hannah said. "Actually, I'm supposed to meet Lacy and Neil Minyard. They should be here soon."

"Did you get a chance to take a look at the Emily Dickinson biography?" Evangeline asked.

"I did. It's interesting. I'm not sure how it helps me, but it's nice to learn more about her."

"Maybe you'll find something if you keep reading. Ah, there they are," Evangeline said as the Minyards' black pickup drove into the parking lot.

The couple climbed out of the truck and waved on their way across the parking lot. Lacy was dressed for the farm in cargo shorts and a loose T-shirt, while Neil wore khakis and a collared shirt, so Hannah guessed he was heading to the bookstore after this.

"Good morning," Evangeline said as they walked inside. "It's fun to have a crowd so early in the day."

"Hi, Evangeline." Lacy said.

"I'm guessing what brings you here is something to do with that poem?" Evangeline asked.

"Sort of," Hannah said. "Apparently it's something to do with the keys that came with the poem."

"We're headed for the local history collection," Neil announced, pointing to a room that branched off the main circulation desk area. "Is it okay if we go in and dig around?"

"Be my guests," Evangeline said. "Let me know if you need anything."

"Will do." Neil led Hannah and Lacy across the lobby and opened the door to the local collections area. He flipped a light switch, and the overhead fluorescents buzzed to life. A small table filled the middle of the room, while bookshelves took up two walls. Filing cabinets and different cabinets with large, flat drawers occupied the other two walls. There were stacks of letters and old journals in a bin tucked onto one of the shelves.

Neil started toward one of the cabinets with wide, flat drawers. "I was in here looking at—"

"Let me guess. Maps?" Lacy said, a smile on her face.

"Yes, maps." Neil shrugged. "I like maps. Anyway, there's all kinds of things in here. Most of the maps are of the local area, but there are some from farther afield. About six months ago, I was looking for a map of voting districts in Kentucky in the 1940s—"

"You get into the most random stuff," Lacy said fondly.

"It had to do with a book I was reading. It was historical fiction, and there was a plot point that hinged on the results of a local election. But the district the author had given was the modern voting district, and I was pretty sure the borders had changed since the forties. They change every ten years after the census."

"Oh no. Don't get started on gerrymandering or we'll be here all day," Lacy said, laughing.

"But it's so interesting to see how the congressional districts change over time because of gerrymandering," Neil protested. "It's a fascinating lens into—"

"You are such a nerd, and I totally love you for it, but for now, can we please focus on the map you brought us here to see?" Lacy asked.

Hannah loved to watch them interact. Though they were teasing each other, it was done in love, and it was clear how much Lacy adored Neil, and how much Neil adored... well, maps, but also Lacy.

"However, we do have other things to do today, so I'll skip the lecture for now. Anyway, I was rooting through this drawer here." He pulled out a thin tray and began thumbing through the contents. "I found several maps from company towns back in the day."

"Such as company towns for coal mining?" Hannah asked. In coal country, the companies that owned the mines had often built whole towns for their employees and their families. All the houses, schools, stores—everything had been owned by the coal company, which allowed the workers and their families to live close to the mines. It gave them a monopoly on prices at the stores, making even more money off the backs of the workers.

"Exactly. Now, if you want to spend some time in history, study the evolution of the coal-mining industry over the last century. Eastern Kentucky sat on some of the biggest deposits of coal in the nation, and that whole area's economy was built around the extraction of coal. There's a great museum over in Benham that explores the history."

"Your grandmother grew up over that way, didn't she, Lacy?" Hannah asked.

"That's right," Lacy said. "It sounds like it was a hard life."

"I think it was," Neil said. "The coal companies made a ton of money, but I think most of the workers had a rough time. The height of the coal industry's power was during and shortly after the Depression, when so many men were grateful to have jobs at all, but it wasn't like they were getting rich. From what I've read, it sounds like most families were barely scraping by. Plus, living in the vicinity of the coal mines meant the air wasn't clean, which caused a lot of health problems for the workers and their families. And it was hardly safe work. Mines could collapse, trapping workers underground."

"Even now you hear of mine accidents where miners are trapped or even killed underground," Hannah said. "I imagine it was worse back then."

"Definitely," Neil said. "Sometimes the workers would organize and go on strike, but they didn't always have the power to do much about their circumstances. Here it is." He tugged the map out of the drawer and laid it on the table. "This is an elevation map," Neil said, pointing to the series of misshapen concentric circles that radiated out from what Hannah assumed were mountaintops. "So you can tell how steep a hill is by how close together the lines of the circles are."

"Right," Hannah acknowledged. She'd seen elevation maps before.

"And the lines here," Neil said, indicating straight lines that formed a border around the hilly area, "mark the boundaries of the company's holdings."

"Which company is that?" Lacy asked.

"The Russell Mining Company." He tapped the top of the map, which said *Russell Mining Company*.

"Oh," Hannah said. She saw what Neil had seen, what had made him think this map might have something to do with the keys. "Oh my goodness."

This map was the key after all.

Chapter Fourteen

Hannah stared at the top of the map. Next to the name Russell Mining Company, there was a small, stylized symbol of a mountain. "Do you have that key on you, Lacy?"

"Neil told me to bring it," Lacy said, retrieving the heavy key from her bag. She set it down on the map, and it thunked against the hard table. "And now I see why."

The mountain symbol on the map was identical to the symbol on the keys.

"Does this mean the keys are connected to the Russell Mining Company somehow?" Lacy asked.

"I suppose that's the logical conclusion." Hannah pulled out her phone and began a search for Russell Mining Company. She clicked on the first link. Along with the history of the business, there were pictures of the company town in its heyday, with rows and rows of identical white shacks along a sloping field. There was also a current photo, which showed mostly a grassy field with a few buildings remaining.

As she scrolled, she saw the symbol on the page. "It says here this is the company's logo," Hannah said, holding it out.

"That makes sense, I guess," Lacy said, "For it to be here on the map anyway."

"Why a mountain?" Hannah asked.

"The mining all happened inside the mountains, and a mountain probably seemed like a nicer thing to put on a logo than a cart full of coal," Neil said.

"I suppose it's better than a pickax or a gas mask," Lacy added.

"A mountain must have been seen as good branding," Neil said. "Mountains are wholesome and natural. Never mind that that was the opposite of life in a coal-mining camp."

"I didn't realize companies even had logos back then, but I guess it does make sense," Hannah said. "But when was this map made?"

Neil showed her a date in the corner, next to the copyright symbol. "In 1938. And companies definitely used logos then. The use of logos started during the Victorian era, when mass-production… Sorry, never mind." He chuckled. "Yes, logos were common."

"And I suppose a mountain is a logical symbol," Hannah said. "Since most of that part of the state is in the Appalachian Mountains."

"And most of the mines are in coal seams deep under the mountains," Neil added. "A mountain symbol makes sense."

"Where exactly are these mines?" Lacy asked. "I mean, where was the Russell Mining Company located?"

"Russell, Kentucky," Hannah said, reading from the website page. "Which looks like it's outside of Harlan, Kentucky, in Harlan County." She turned to Lacy. "Russell Mining Company is where your grandmother's father worked, right? Where she grew up?"

"I think that's right," Lacy said, shaking her head. "Okay, I need to call my mom. Hang on."

She took out her phone and called Christine. Hannah only heard one end of the conversation, but she could follow it well enough.

"Hi, Mom. We're at the library, and we found something odd. Your grandfather worked for Russell Mining Company, right?... Wait, *he* did too?... Because Neil found a map in the local history room, and it shows the holdings of Russell Mining Company, and it has the same symbol that's on the key.... I know, that's why we're so confused.... Okay, I'll see you soon."

Lacy hung up and turned to Hannah and Neil. "Mom wants to see it. She's on her way. She'll be here in ten minutes."

Neil leaned forward to study the map again, and Lacy wandered off to look at other things on the shelves, so Hannah turned her attention to the website on her phone to read more about the Russell Mining Company. The company was founded in 1907, buying up land along a seam in the coal-rich hills of eastern Kentucky. The company developed a town around the mine, and at its height more than five hundred employees lived there with their families, which was named Russell.

The beginning of World War I initiated a boom in the coal industry, which was when much of the infrastructure of the town was developed and recruiting ramped up, but the end of the war ushered in a bust, and the Great Depression only exacerbated it. The company laid off half its workforce during that time, leaving the miners and their families homeless as well as jobless. But America's entry into World War II brought a great demand for coal, and the town and the mines expanded during the war and the postwar years. The push for mechanization in the 1950s, and then the Korean War, expanded things even further, but then railroads and the government started shifting from coal to gas in the 1960s, and the industry declined significantly.

The company shut down and the mine was shuttered in 1965. There had been a significant accident in the mines in 1943, when part of one of the shafts collapsed and three men were killed.

Hannah was distracted from the tragic history when Christine joined them.

"Hi," Lacy's mom said cheerfully. "Thanks for calling me. I need to see this."

"There's the map Neil found," Lacy said, gesturing to the table. "As you can see, the symbol on the keys is a perfect match for the company's logo." She slid a yearbook she'd been flipping through into its place on the shelf.

"That's incredible," Christine said, bending forward to study the map. She glanced between Lacy's key and the symbol on the map. "How did you find this, Neil?"

"I saw it when I was looking through these maps a while ago," Neil explained.

"I wish I could remember half of what you're able to. But thank you for finding this." Christine straightened. "Yes, Russell was the company where Grandpa worked. So did all of my uncles, and my dad before we moved to Lexington."

"That's right." Hannah remembered that part of the history.

"My dad had seen the mines destroy so many men," Christine said. "It was impossibly hard going down into the mines every day. Breathing the dust that ruined your lungs. Tethering families to poverty and dependence on the company. He had grown up with it and didn't want it for himself or his family, so he saved every penny he could and got us out of there. Of course, the mines closed permanently when I was still a kid, so it was an especially good thing we'd left and found something else."

"Do you remember Russell at all?" Neil asked.

"I don't remember living there. But we went back to visit early, since both sides of the family were there. I was young, but even I could tell that things were bleak. And then once the mine closed, most people went from being poor to absolute destitution. There simply weren't other jobs in the area. When the mines closed, so did the towns. Grandma and Grandpa had been able to save up enough to buy a piece of land nearby and build a house, but most people weren't that lucky. I remember seeing these shacks all along the hillsides. Not that we were living the high life over in Lexington, but at least I never went without food or electricity."

"Do you still have family out that way?" Hannah asked. Whoever sent the key clearly had a connection to the Russell Mining Company.

"Not that I know of," Christine said. "My parents have both passed away, as you know. My grandmother on my mom's side died when I was still in middle school, and my grandpa when I was even younger. We stopped visiting after that."

"What about your dad's side of the family? They were from Russell too, right?"

"They were all long gone. Like I said, it was a hard life. And even those who survived had health problems afterward. Black lung got so many of them when they were still in the prime of their lives."

"But then who could have sent the keys if there was no one left?" Lacy had obviously been following Hannah's train of thought.

Christine shrugged. "I don't know. I wish Mom were here. She would be able to help."

"What about Nancy?" Hannah said, recalling the name. "Your grandma's sister?"

"I imagine she probably passed away too," Christine said.

"You don't know for sure?" Lacy asked.

"I never met her," Christine said. "Like I said, she and my mom had a falling-out of some kind. They never spoke again, as far as I know. Mom wouldn't talk about her. Nancy was never a part of my life, and I can't see how or why she would be sending us packages now. Even if by some miracle she was still alive, I don't know how she'd find me or even know Lacy existed."

"And if she wanted to reach out after all this time, why not start with hello, instead of these cryptic packages?" Lacy added.

"It must be someone with a connection to Russell, though. Who else could it be?" Hannah tried to make sense of it and couldn't. But a moment later, she thought of something. "Madison is from eastern Kentucky."

"She is?" Lacy asked.

"Who's Madison?" Christine added.

Hannah quickly explained to Christine that Madison was the one who had dropped the package in her mailbox, and that she'd been researching the younger woman and trying to find a connection.

"Where in eastern Kentucky is she from?" Lacy asked.

"Harlan," Hannah said.

"That's not too far from Russell," Christine said.

"Maybe she's connected to your family somehow," Lacy said. "What if she's Nancy's granddaughter, here to make contact with her grandma's sister's side of the family?"

"Then why didn't she do that?" Neil asked. "She was here. If that was her plan, why not stop in at the farm and introduce herself? She had your address."

"You ruin all my best ideas," Lacy complained.

Hannah stifled a laugh. She appreciated Neil's voice of reason. He was the string to Lacy's kite, keeping her grounded.

"But Madison must be connected to your family somehow, if she's from the same part of the state and dropped off the packages," Neil said. "The question is how?"

"I don't know," Christine said.

"Then we need to find out more about her," Lacy said.

"Luckily, that was my plan for this morning anyway," Hannah said. "I learned her name last night. The internet wasn't helpful, but I thought I would spend some time poking around the library databases today to see if I could find anything else."

"Oh man. I wish I could help with that," Lacy said, "but I have to get back. I have a delivery in an hour."

"It sounds like a lot of fun to me," Neil said. "But the store opens in fifteen minutes, so I've got to get over there."

"I've got nothing but time," Christine said. "Need any help?"

"I'd appreciate it." Christine would know many more family connections than Hannah.

"Come on, Neil," Lacy said. "I'll drop you at the bookstore before I head home."

Neil reluctantly slid the map into the drawer and closed it. "Please do keep us posted."

"I will," Hannah promised. "And thank you, Neil. I don't know how you were able to connect the symbol on the key to a logo you saw six months ago, but I'm grateful."

"Unfortunately, all it did was lead to more questions," Neil said.

"It's getting us closer to the truth," Hannah said. "We just need to keep digging."

Lacy and Neil left, and a few minutes later, Hannah and Christine were seated at neighboring computer terminals.

"Where should we begin?" Christine asked.

"I was thinking I would start with vital records for Harlan County," Hannah said. Such records were public, and they could be a wealth of information about a person's life. Usually they were collected by counties, and many counties had put their records in searchable databases that could be accessed online or at libraries. "If Madison was born there, hopefully I'll be able to find her birth certificate. Maybe that will tell me something, such as the names of her parents."

"In that case, I'll try a genealogy site and see if anything comes up for her name there," Christine said.

"You can do that here?"

"As long as you're using the library computer, you can access this one for free," Christine said, selecting a logo on the desktop. A webpage popped up, and Christine entered credentials that proved she'd done this before. "Frank had always heard that one of his ancestors was part Cherokee, and he wanted to know whether it was true or not."

"Was it?"

"Sadly, no. Just regular old Irish who came over during the potato famine, it turns out. Frank never had much tolerance for fancy, so he was glad to have the truth so he could put the rumor to bed."

"Well, let me know what you find out about Madison."

"I will." Christine turned to her screen.

Hannah poked around for a minute, but if the database was here, it wasn't obvious. "I'll be right back," she told Christine as she got up.

Evangeline was shelving books in the biography section when Hannah found her. "What can I do for you?"

"I was hoping to search for some vital records," Hannah said. "Would you be able to help me figure out where to do that?"

"Fun. I love vital records." Evangeline slid a biography on Winston Churchill into place.

"Really?" Hannah didn't see what was so fun about them.

"Sure. You can learn so much about a person's story from government records—when they were born and where, who they married and when, how many children they had, whether they bought property, when they died—you can get the rough outline of a whole life. Come on, I'll show you."

Hannah led her to the computer she was using, and Evangeline gave directions to navigate to a database that searched records throughout the state of Kentucky. "Do you know which county you want to search?"

"Harlan," Hannah said.

"Okay. Select the county from the menu here, and then type the person's name in this field. You can also filter by type of record if you want."

Hannah typed in *Madison Maris* and selected Harlan County.

"I had a feeling that might be who you wanted," Evangeline said. "Let's see what comes up."

Hannah ran the search, and a message popped up on the screen: *No Results*.

"So obviously she hasn't died or been married in Harlan County," Evangeline said. "But she must not have been born there either."

"Which means that I would have to search every county in Kentucky to find out where she was born," Hannah said.

"If she was born in Kentucky at all," Evangeline said. "Other states have different systems."

Madison had called eastern Kentucky home in the student newspaper, so it made sense to start with other counties in that part of the state. But she could have been born anywhere and moved there when she was young.

Hannah was nearly overwhelmed by the sudden enormity of the task ahead, but she didn't see any alternative. "I guess I've got to keep searching."

"Maybe not," Christine said from the chair beside her. "I think I found her."

Chapter Fifteen

*Y*ou did?" Hannah leaned over to see Christine's computer screen, and Evangeline craned her neck as well.

"This family tree was created by a Rachel Holtzman, who appears to be Madison's aunt," Christine said. "She's tracing her family tree, but she filled out the generation she is part of and their children. See, here's Rachel and her sister, Danielle Maris. They were both born with the last name Hammer, but Danielle married Brian Maris—" She pointed at the screen. "And they have two kids, Caleb and Madison. This Madison was born at the right time to be the girl we're looking for."

Hannah quicky scribbled the names Christine had found. "You're a genius, Christine."

"It's amazing what you can find out using this thing," Christine said, but she was clearly pleased by the praise.

"Is there any connection to you and Lacy?"

"Not that I can tell," Christine said. "If she's related to us, it's so far back that it's not showing up on her family tree, or on ours."

Whether Madison was a relative or not, she was obviously still connected. Hannah needed to figure out how.

Hannah was already typing the name *Brian Maris* into a browser window. "How about I research Brian, and you research Danielle?"

"Sounds great. What are we looking for exactly?"

"Anything that tells us how to get in touch with them or Madison, and how Madison is connected to any of this."

"I'll leave you both to it," Evangeline said. "But you must tell me what you figure out."

"We will," Christine promised.

It didn't take long for Hannah to find a listing for Brian Maris on the website for a law firm, Maris and Maris. Brian and his brother, Craig, ran the firm together, according to the page, and they handled all kinds of family, estate, real estate, contracts, and tax cases.

"Madison's dad is a lawyer," Hannah said.

Christine peered at the screen. "That's a lot of different kinds of law."

"I guess there are two of them, so maybe they divide and conquer?"

"It sounds like a small-town kind of law firm," Christine said. "Odds are they're the only game in town, so they work on whatever comes up. Karen DiSalvo is like that. Doesn't matter if you want to buy a house, adopt a child, or change your will, she can handle it for you. Her office is above Jump Start if you ever need her."

"Good to know."

"Where is the fine law firm of Maris and Maris located?" Christine asked.

Hannah opened the Contact Us page. "Harlan, Kentucky." She copied the address.

"You should send them an email," Christine said, indicating a contact form that took up most of the page.

"I'm not sure what I'd say," Hannah said. "'Hi, I'm wondering why your daughter has a strange fascination with keys and Emily Dickinson?'"

"I'm sure you could come up with something slightly better than that if you tried," Christine said, in the same gently chastising tone she'd used so many times when Hannah and Lacy had come up with some harebrained plan as children—like the time they'd decided to give Lacy's family dog a makeover with Christine's makeup and hair ties.

"Let me think about it," Hannah said. "For now, I'm going to see what else I can find."

She returned to the search results. Brian had been quoted in a newsletter that appeared to be meant for other Kentucky lawyers, discussing the particularities of handling an out-of-state adoption. He had completed several five-kilometer runs, and his finish times were posted online. He had donated to multiple charities, and his name was listed on their donor pages. No social media, as far as she could tell. There was nothing else useful that she could see.

Still, there was more she could learn. She went back to the vital records database and ran a search for Brian's name in Harlan County. According to a property record, he'd bought a house with Danielle Maris in Harlan County nearly twenty years before. There was no record of a home being sold, before or after that date, or of a marriage, death, or birth. Their purchase of this house must have occurred when the family had moved to the county, but from where? Hannah wasn't sure if it mattered. However, some quick math indicated that they had moved when Madison was young, probably a toddler. That explained why there was no birth certificate for her in Harlan County.

Hannah ran an internet search for the street address from the property record. A real estate site said the property wasn't for sale, but showed photos of a two-story house with a mansard-style roof and a fanciful cupola on top. It was located out in the country, surrounded by thirty acres of woods, a stream, and a pond.

That was the house where Madison had grown up. And presumably where she lived now, if she'd returned home after college. Which was nice, but how did this connect to the poem, the key, and the handkerchief? What was the tie that bound Madison to Lacy and Hannah?

"Do you recognize this house?" Hannah asked Christine.

"I do."

Hannah felt her heartbeat speed up. This was it. This was the connection. "How?"

"I've spent the last several minutes clicking through photos of the interior on Danielle's website." Christine pointed to the webpage on her screen, which was titled DANIELLE MARIS, INTERIOR DESIGNER. "She does good work, if her pictures are anything to go by."

Christine clicked on the Gallery tab, and a picture of the exterior of the house appeared, followed by photos of the interior, featuring wide plank floors, milled woodwork, gauzy curtains, and lots of white paint.

"It's a nice house, but I don't know why I'd need to pay someone to tell me to paint everything white," Christine said.

Hannah laughed. "I think it's kind of nice. It looks clean, open, and airy that way. Besides, we've found the family we were searching for." But now, what did she do with the information? She hadn't found any connection to Christine and Lacy.

"I need to get going," Christine said, stretching her arms above her head. "I'm supposed to meet Melba for lunch soon."

Goodness. Was it lunchtime already? Hannah checked her watch. No, she still had some time. Christine must be heading for an early lunch.

"Thank you for your help," Hannah said.

"I think you have it backward," Christine said. "You're helping me, remember?"

"It feels pretty mutual at this point," Hannah said. "I want to find out what's going on as much as you do. Can I see that key one more time?"

"Why don't you take the whole package for a while? I feel like you'll be able to do more with it than I can." Christine pulled the envelope out of her bag and held it out for Hannah.

"Are you sure?"

"Absolutely. That way you can reference whatever you need to, whenever you want."

"Thank you. I'll take good care of it."

"I have no doubt." Christine waved as she headed out.

There was one more thing Hannah wanted to check before she went to the restaurant. One person kept coming up in this search. Someone they hadn't looked into yet, who had lived in Russell and grown up in a family with ties to the Russell Mining Company. One person who was a big question mark in this whole mystery.

Hannah opened a new browser window and searched for the name *Nancy Whitmore*.

The first thing that came up was an obituary from the previous year.

> *Nancy Marie Whitmore died on November 6 at Roaring Brook Village Nursing Home in Harlan, Kentucky. Born on January 5, 1940, she grew up in Russell, Kentucky, and spent most of her adult life there. She is remembered for her wit, her kind smile, and her love of laughter. A memorial service will be held at Morris Funeral Home on Saturday, November 9.*

That was it. That was the whole obituary. There was no next of kin identified. No survivors. No one, seemingly, who would miss her.

She went back to the vital records search again and looked for records for Nancy in Harlan County. A birth certificate popped up, but showed nothing surprising. The dates and names all matched what Hannah expected to see. There was also a death certificate. The details matched the information in the obituary, and the cause of death was listed as heart failure. Not all that surprising, though still tragic.

There was no marriage certificate registered in Harlan County, and no birth certificates citing Nancy beyond her own. It seemed as though she'd stayed pretty close to home throughout her life, and it appeared likely that she'd never married or had children.

There was one interesting record, though. On October 30, 1972, a property in Russell, Kentucky, was transferred to Nancy's name. There was no purchase listed, no mortgage taken out on the property, just a transfer. Hannah did some quick math. Given when Christine said her grandparents had passed away, this must be a record of Nancy assuming ownership of her parents' house. The one they had built, according to Christine, after the Russell mines closed.

Hannah searched the address of the house and saw that it was a modest bungalow with a front porch set on half an acre of rural land. The house had not been sold or listed for sale, at least not that the real estate site recorded. It was fair to assume Nancy had inherited the house and lived in it until she went to the nursing home.

Hannah felt a sense of melancholy over the fact that Lacy's family didn't know this woman or this history. This was Christine's aunt. How did they not know anything about her? What had happened between the sisters to drive them apart so thoroughly and completely? What had driven their lives in separate directions, never to meet again?

Hannah couldn't imagine anything bad enough that she would cut off her brother and never speak to him again. No matter how many bad surprise dates he threw at her, Drew was the one who had been there with her in childhood, sharing games and long car rides and whispered conversation on Christmas Eve as they tried to wait up for Santa. Drew was the only one who truly understood so many parts of what had made Hannah who she was, and who had loved Mom the way she did.

She wondered if Nancy regretted whatever had happened, whether she missed her sister once she was gone, whether she'd ever tried to reconcile. Nancy had outlived Helen by several years. Did she even know that her sister had died?

There was no way to know. But whatever else was true, Hannah knew that Nancy had died more than seven months ago. She couldn't have been behind the packages Madison delivered.

And yet the Emily Dickinson poem that had been in Christine's package was about how the bond between friends was still strong, even when they were separated. Even if something had hurt the relationship. The theme was too close to what had happened to the sisters to be a coincidence. Was the poem a clue about sisters long separated? Was it about regret? A plea? She had no idea.

Hannah closed out of the database and pushed herself to her feet. She might not know how the poem fit in, but she knew so much more now than she had when she'd walked into the library today. She knew the keys were somehow connected to the Russell Mining Company, which strongly suggested that the envelopes had been sent by someone with ties to Helen's family, who had lived in Russell and worked in the mines.

She needed to read more of Helen's journals to find out more about her relationship with her sister, but Hannah had uncovered an address for Madison, as well as some information about her parents. She had learned that Nancy, Helen's sister, inherited the house her parents built, but she never married, never had kids, and died in a nursing home with no family to speak of.

Christine had said that there was no link between her family tree and Madison's, so how were all these pieces of information con-nected? Hannah knew Madison was involved. She knew there was a connection to the Russell Mining Company. The handkerchiefs had an *M* embroidered on them. Someone liked an Emily Dickinson poem that might have made them think of the sisters. Or was she extrapolating too much there? Was she so desperate for answers that she was seeing a link where none existed?

She didn't know. The more answers she got, the more confused she grew.

Chapter Sixteen

Friday afternoon, Hannah unlocked the restaurant and flipped on the lights. She had come in a little earlier than normal to work on her recipe for Kentucky Hot Browns, but when she tried to get to work, she realized she was still distracted by all that had happened at the library that morning.

She walked into the dining room, took the chairs off one of the tables, and spread the contents of Christine's envelope out on the surface. There had to be something she was missing.

First she picked up the paper with the poem.

Long Years apart — can make no
Breach a second cannot fill —

Now that she knew what the full poem said, it was a bit easier to figure out which words were supposed to be on the faded paper. She knew it was about estrangement, but she still didn't know why it had been included. What did it have to do with the key and the handkerchief, and why had it been sent to Christine, but not Lacy?

Setting aside the poem, she moved on to the handkerchief, running her fingers along its lacy scalloped edge and then over the blue thread that spelled out the *M*. It had clearly been done by hand. A machine's stitches would be smooth and even, while the stitches here were of varying lengths and directions. Plus, the letter *M* was crooked. The embroidery was certainly better than Hannah could have produced, but the stitches didn't appear to be the work of someone with a lot of skill or practice at embroidery. Which meant…what?

Hannah set the handkerchief aside and picked up the brass key, turning it over in her hands. She studied the mountain logo carved into the metal. It was a connection to eastern Kentucky, to coal mining, to the Russell Mining Company and the town of Russell, and likely to Helen's family in some way—that was the only tie Lacy and Christine had to the town. But exactly who were they connected to, and how?

Now that she knew about the connection, Hannah knew she needed to keep reading Helen's diaries. Maybe there was some clue buried in those pages that would help her make sense of it all.

And she had to talk to Madison. Whether the young woman knew everything that was going on or not, she was squarely in the middle of this whole thing, which meant she certainly knew more than Hannah did.

Should she also call the law firm of Maris & Maris? She decided she'd only do that if she got desperate. If Madison's involvement with the packages had nothing to do with her family's law firm, Hannah's call would confuse them and possibly get Madison in trouble. If the young woman hadn't done anything wrong, Hannah didn't want that. Besides, she doubted the law firm would simply hand out information about its employees' families to anyone who asked. They'd probably consider that information confidential and privileged.

For now, though, she needed to focus on her restaurant. It was Friday night, so they'd likely be busy. She could help Jacob by prepping vegetables or shaping hamburger patties, but right now, while it was quiet, maybe she had a moment to try tweaking that Hot Browns recipe. They would be serving the dish tonight anyway, so she would be prepping the ingredients and would get a chance to try her changes. The traditional recipe for the open-faced sandwich, created in the 1920s by a chef at the Brown Hotel in Louisville, was delicious, but she was eager to make it her own.

She gathered the traditional ingredients—strips of thick-cut bacon, roasted turkey breast, fresh bread. The original recipe called for white bread, but Hannah thought starting with good bread made all the difference in how the sandwich turned out. She also took a small bowl of her secret ingredient out of the fridge and set it on the counter to come to room temperature while she prepared the rest of the ingredients.

Hannah started by warming up the slices of turkey and cooking the night's bacon. The rest of the bacon would be reheated when it was time to serve it in the dining room. Then she pulled out a pan and heated butter and flour, stirring them together over low heat until the flour browned. She added milk, a bit at a time, and salt and pepper. At this point it was a traditional béchamel sauce, but once all the milk had been added and the sauce was the right temperature, she added the egg yolk that would make it so rich. She also added shredded parmesan and cheddar cheese to make a Mornay sauce, finishing with a touch of nutmeg and a dash of hot sauce.

Jacob came in, tying his apron over his clothes, while she was chopping tomatoes and parsley. "It smells good in here," he said. "You cooked bacon."

"Guilty," she said. "It's all ready for tonight."

"And you made the Mornay sauce for the Hot Browns?" he asked, nodding at the pan on the stove. "Do I get to try it?"

"You bet. I'll need your opinion."

"Sounds good." He set to work shaping the grass-fed ground beef into hamburger patties.

Meanwhile, she grilled a few tomatoes then grated more parmesan and cheddar cheese. Once everything was ready, she placed a slice of bread on the sheet pan, topped it with a grilled tomato slice and some turkey, covered the whole thing in Mornay sauce, and topped it with more cheese. Then she slid the pan into the oven, which had been set to broil, and let the dish cook until the cheese was brown and the sauce was hot and bubbling. She pulled out the open-faced sandwich and finished it by adding two strips of bacon, a touch of chopped parsley, and her secret ingredient—a drizzle of the blackberry compote she'd made earlier in the week.

She cut the sandwich in half, put the halves on two plates, and handed one to Jacob.

He washed his hands and accepted the plate. Hannah took a clean knife and fork and cut into her sandwich.

"Oh wow," Jacob said, swallowing a bite. "The blackberry compote is amazing. It adds such an unexpected kick."

"You like it?" She took a bite herself, and loved how the sweetness and the tartness of the blackberry sauce balanced out the salty bacon and the rich Mornay sauce. It was even better than she'd hoped. Maybe this would become a signature dish.

"Love it." He took another bite and chewed, and then tilted his head thoughtfully.

"What?" Hannah asked.

"It's delicious. But you know how you're always reminding me to think about what our customers will want?"

"Of course." As much as she enjoyed creating high-end dishes, Hannah knew that her customers in small-town Kentucky weren't likely to embrace the kind of food she'd been used to preparing in LA, and she'd had to remind Jacob—who enjoyed the kinds of foods she did—to keep their customers in mind when he prepared dishes.

"I love this combo, but I wonder if it might be a bit more than people around here will go for. The Hot Brown sells well enough as it is. Do we need to add the compote? Will the customers want it that way?"

"That's a good point. I don't know. Maybe I'll have a few people try it and see what they think. I know Marshall's review dinged us for the decorative swirls you like to add on a plate, but I wonder if that would be a good way to give customers the option to enjoy the compote without committing to it on the whole sandwich. They'd be able to dip individual bites in it that way."

"You know, I like that idea." He cut off another bite.

Dad would be a good gauge. Uncle Gordon too. They were representative of the people in this town. And she was sure she could find a few other willing taste testers. She finished her sandwich and washed her plate.

She grabbed peppers, zucchini, fresh herbs, and a sharp knife to help with prep.

While she chopped, her mind returned—as it always seemed to these days—to the mysterious packages and what she'd learned that morning. Hannah couldn't shake the feeling that Nancy Whitmore was involved in this somehow. Nancy had the sole direct tie to Russell Mining Company. Sure, she was dead, but did that mean she couldn't have sent packages to relatives she'd never met and might not even know existed?

Hannah finished slicing a red pepper and set that theory aside along with it. She sounded crazy, even to herself. The packages could not have come from Christine's late aunt. And Nancy wasn't the only tie to Russell Mining Company. Helen was raised there and married a man who also had grown up in Russell. But they had been dead even longer than Nancy, so how could they possibly be involved? On the other hand, Madison was definitely involved. They knew that for sure. But what was her tie to Russell, and to Christine and Lacy?

Her mind kept circling back to Nancy, the greatest unknown in all of this. Maybe it was the Emily Dickinson connection. Hannah didn't know whether Nancy, like Dickinson, was a poet or would be posthumously recognized as a genius, but she did know that, like Dickinson, Nancy had never married or had children.

Why had she stayed in her hometown when her sister had fled? Had she wanted to marry? Had she ever known love? According to the biography, Dickinson was rumored to have had many loves in her life, but there wasn't concrete evidence to support serious interest in a particular suitor.

Hannah got a sinking feeling. Was she going to end up like Emily Dickinson, scribbling recipes in an attic, refusing to come out of her room, turning up her nose at all the men who came to call? Would they someday stop calling? Why was she even thinking about dating in terms of *coming to call* anyway? She wasn't from Emily Dickinson's time, when men would stop by the parlor during calling hours to express their interest. But though the term was outdated, it didn't feel all that different from what Mitch and Ollie had done, to be honest.

In any case, Hannah *did* want to marry and have children someday. It was just that she didn't feel like she had time for a relationship at this moment in her life. If she wanted the Hot Spot to be successful, it had to be her focus.

But by pushing away the men who had expressed interest in her since her move, was she dooming herself to a life of spinsterhood?

She hit the brakes on this train of thought. No one even used the word spinster anymore. She wasn't Emily Dickinson. She was seriously starting to lose it.

Still, though, now that she thought about it, she wondered if she'd been too hasty in closing the door on Mitch, on Raquel's cousin, and on Ollie. Well, not Ollie. He was not for her.

She started to wonder whether she had been too hasty in deciding she wasn't open to meeting *anyone*. How else was she supposed to find the man she would want to marry?

"Hey, Hannah?" Elaine popped her head into the kitchen, a smile on her face. "Liam is here to see you." She winked and ducked out into the dining room.

They weren't even open yet. What was Liam doing here? Hannah set down her knife, washed her hands, smoothed her hair, and took a deep breath before she followed.

Out in the front of the house, Dylan and Raquel were getting the dining room ready, setting down chairs, lighting candles, and rolling silverware. Through the front windows, Hannah could see that the clouds had grown thick and dark, hugging the tops of the hills. Even in here, with the air conditioners blasting, the air felt dense and close. It would storm soon.

When she saw Liam standing by the door, something inside her flipped. He really was very handsome. He smiled when he saw her and held out his hands.

Which was when she noticed he was holding her pie plate.

"I came by to return this," he said.

She forced herself to smile, feeling ridiculous. "What did you think of the pie?"

"It's neck and neck with my grandma's," he said. "I can't make up my mind which is better. I kept eating more, hoping it would become clear, but I might need you to make me another one so I can decide."

"Nice try." She took the pie plate with a chuckle. "I'm glad you enjoyed it, though." Then she had an idea. "How do you feel about Kentucky Hot Browns?"

"Love them," he replied without hesitation.

"I'm working on a new twist, and I need taste testers. Would you be willing to offer your services?"

"Let's see. Would I be willing to try a new twist on one of my favorite dishes from the best chef in town?" He pretended to consider it for a moment. "Sure, I suppose I can make the sacrifice."

"Great. Have a seat anywhere. I'll be right back." Hannah returned to the kitchen and set the pie plate on the counter. "We have our first taste tester," she told Jacob.

"I didn't realize being fire chief came with so many perks," Jacob said with a knowing glance.

"I need someone to try the recipe, and he's here," she said. "There is nothing more to it than that, so you can wipe that smirk off your face."

Jacob snorted as he went back to searing chicken in a skillet.

She ignored him and started making the dish again. A few minutes later, she drizzled compote over the piping-hot sandwich and carried the plate out of the kitchen. She found Liam at the table where she'd left the items from Christine's package. Raquel swung past with a roll of clean silverware.

"I'm sorry about that stuff," Hannah said, setting the plate in front of him. "I was going to put it away before we opened."

"It's no problem," he said. "This is that key you were asking about on Sunday, right?"

"It is." That explained why he'd chosen this table, of all the free seats at the restaurant. She'd told Liam and Ryder about the keys and handkerchief and poem at church, when she'd asked them whether there was anything in the hills the key might unlock. "I still don't know what it unlocks, but now I'm pretty sure it's nothing around here. I think it has something to do with coal mining."

"So maybe it *is* an abandoned mine? That's even creepier than caves."

"I seriously hope not." She pointed at the food on his plate. "You should try that before it gets cold."

Liam unrolled his napkin. "What's that on top?"

"It's a blackberry compote," she told him.

"I've never seen a Hot Brown with that," he said. "This must be the twist you mentioned." He cut a bite, making sure to get all the ingredients then lifted it to his nose.

"You're taking this taste test very seriously," Hannah said as he inhaled deeply.

"Food is no joking matter, and it means a lot to me that you want my input about something for your business. This is serious for you, so it's serious for me." He closed his eyes and put the morsel in his mouth. His eyes flew wide open again. "Wow." He chewed quickly and swallowed. "That's really good."

"You like it?"

His mouth was already full with a second, larger bite, but his enthusiastic nod was all the reassurance she needed.

"Would you order it if it was on the menu?"

"Now that I've tried it, yes. But if I'd read the description and it said there was a blackberry sauce? Probably not, honestly. You may need to give folks a chance to taste it. Once they try it, they're going to realize it's delicious, but they may be hesitant otherwise."

"Those are good notes," Hannah said. "I'll have to think about that."

"I'll tell people how good it is," he said. "If you pay me in more of these."

She laughed. "We'll have to see."

Liam took another bite, and his gaze drifted over the poem. "This is the paper you mentioned?"

"It is indeed," Hannah said. "I found out it's a poem by Emily Dickinson."

Liam examined it. "I guess the dashes should have given that away, but it's not one of the more famous ones."

Hannah tried to not let her surprise show. She didn't realize the fire chief knew anything about poetry. But then she remembered that his grandmother had been the head librarian many years before. He'd probably spent as much time at that library as she had, if not more.

"It's not. The full poem is here." She pulled up a website showing the full text of the poem on her phone.

Liam popped another bite in his mouth and read the poem as he chewed. "Well, that's clear as mud."

"Exactly. And the last piece of the puzzle is that handkerchief."

"I was admiring that while you were in the kitchen, for obvious reasons." He gave her the phone and picked up the handkerchief.

"What do you mean?"

"Well, my full name is William, after all, so obviously I like that it has a *W* on it."

She chuckled. "Oh, given the way it's oriented on the cloth, that's an *M*."

He rotated it on the table. "I mean, I can see that. But it's an odd *M*, don't you think?"

Now that he mentioned it, it did look like a strange version of an *M*, with swoops on both ends of the letter and the loop in the middle point. Usually a script-style capital *M* would only have decorations on the left side of the letter, not on both sides.

"But if you turn it this way," he said, twisting the cloth to its original vantage point, "it's pretty clear that it's a *W*. I think it was stitched onto the fabric upside down." When he held the handkerchief that way, it was suddenly obvious he was right. The swoops on either side of the letter and the loop in the middle clearly indicated a *W*, not an *M*.

"But why is it like that on the handkerchief then?" she asked. But even as she said the words, a potential answer came into her mind. "The stitches are the work of someone who was learning. It's understandable that they might have made such a mistake."

"I don't know about that. Embroidery isn't my thing," he said, shrugging. "But what I do know is that my grandma was really into monograms, and pretty much everything she gave me for most of my life had my initials sewn into it. So I know an embroidered *W* when I see it."

He was right. She didn't know how she hadn't seen it before.

And that was when she realized they'd been looking at the whole thing all wrong.

Chapter Seventeen

I t's a *W*."

"What?" Lacy was outside with the chickens, judging by the sound of soft clucking on her end of the line. "What do you mean?"

"Liam saw the handkerchief and knew it was a *W* immediately. Once he showed it to me from that angle, I couldn't unsee it."

"How did Liam see the handkerchief?"

"Your mom gave me her package to hold on to this morning while I try to figure this thing out. Liam came in to return my pie plate, and he saw it lying there."

"And why did Liam have your pie plate?"

"Because I made him a peach pie as a thank-you." Honestly, everyone acted as if there was more going on with Liam than there was. "Anyway he asked who *W* was. Because his name is William and his grandma was into monograms, he saw it immediately."

"But why would it be positioned like that if it was a *W*? It only makes sense for it to be an *M*. Otherwise the letter would be upside down."

"Apparently it *is* upside down. We saw that the embroidery had been done by someone who didn't know what they were doing. There were all those uneven stitches, and the places where it was clear a thread had been pulled out."

"Fair enough, but would even a beginner get it *that* wrong?"

"Go look at your handkerchief. You'll see."

"Okay, hang on." There was a clanging sound behind Lacy, and then the creak of a gate. "Hennifer, stay in there. Hannah, I'm heading into the house now." The thud of the door echoed behind her. "The envelope is on the table." There was a pause, and then Lacy gasped. "Oh my goodness. It's totally a *W*."

"Right?"

"Now that I see it, I don't know how I missed it. We were looking at it all wrong."

"It's amazing how once you see it, you can't unsee it."

"Now we just need the rest of the mystery to make sense," Lacy said. "So what does it mean if it's a *W*? Who could W be?"

"I started thinking about that, and I suppose there are a few people it could be," Hannah said. "Wasn't your great-grandfather named Walter?"

"He was," Lacy confirmed. "But I doubt he has anything to do with this."

"It's possible," Hannah said. "But there's a more obvious answer, which I think is more likely to be right."

"Whitmore," Lacy said. "Grandma's maiden name was Whitmore."

"Right. So who on your grandmother's side of the family would have made these handkerchiefs?"

"And who was responsible for sending them?"

The skies opened up at the beginning of dinner service on Friday night. Lightning flashed and thunder crashed, and rain sluiced down in sheets. It was an impressive storm, and one Hannah enjoyed watching from inside the restaurant, but the storm passed as quickly as it had come, leaving behind cooler air and pavement that glistened under the streetlights.

The night was busy, and there were groups of people crowding around the door waiting for tables for most of the evening. Hannah couldn't be upset about that, and she was so busy that she didn't have any time to worry about the mystery. The restaurant was full, running it was exhausting and exhilarating, and she was wiped out by the time they had waved their last customer out the door.

When she finally locked up and went upstairs, instead of falling into bed, she settled on the couch with a mug of mint tea and one of Helen's diaries. Helen was a part of this, whatever it was. She hadn't sent those packages from beyond the grave—Hannah was sure about that at least—but the evidence so far indicated that this involved her. This mystery had something to do with Helen, Nancy, and whatever it was that had separated the sisters for so long. The more she thought about it, the more Hannah believed that was what the poem was about.

But what was the issue at the heart of the matter?

The first diary Hannah picked up was from 1953, when Helen would have been fifteen. She cracked open the leather cover and started to read.

Helen's neat handwriting covered the pages. A girl named Felicity had teased Helen for getting a math problem wrong. A fire had broken out in the Blythe house overnight, and everyone in town had shown up to help extinguish it. She'd copied a pineapple upside-down cake recipe from a magazine that she wanted to try making if she could find some canned pineapple.

>*Walter Knicely asked to walk me home from school today. I told him he was welcome to walk with me, but he shouldn't expect me to go steady with him. I'm not going to fall in love and get stuck in this town like everyone else does. I don't care how cute Walter is.*

That was interesting, since Hannah knew she'd ended up marrying Walter Knicely a few years later. Hannah wondered what had happened in the intervening years to change Helen's mind. And how had her correspondence with Bert affected her choice? The letters from Bert were written in 1955, when Helen would have been seventeen. So that was after this diary. Hannah wondered if Helen would mention Bert.

There were difficult entries detailing the times when, near the end of the month, the family ran out of money to spend at the company store.

>*Mama says we can't buy things on credit, no matter how much we're tempted, because the rate they charge is so high that we'll end up paying two or three times what the item is worth by the time we finally pay it off. She says we must make do with what we have, even if it means eating only vegetables for a few days. We have plenty of potatoes. I am so sick of potatoes. Everyone else in town buys on credit, so I don't understand why we can't too.*

Hannah supposed that thriftiness and good financial sense was what had allowed Helen's parents to buy their own piece of land when the mines closed. She hoped Helen had understood that when the time had come.

But the entries that interested Hannah the most were the ones that mentioned Nancy.

Nancy dared me to climb a tall tree this afternoon. I didn't want to risk falling and getting hurt, so Nancy said I was "pigeon-livered and lacked gall." She has been reading Shakespeare, so I'm sure that's a quote from one play or another. Dad says reading so many books will ruin her mind.

Nancy wore my blouse today, and she didn't even ask. She kept it hidden under her coat until we were at school and it was too late for me to tell her to go back and change. She infuriates me.

Nancy asked me if I would read her essay before she turned it in for English class, and I have to admit, it was pretty good. She may be annoying, but she's a good writer.

None of this told Hannah what had driven the sisters apart, what happened to Nancy, or what any of it had to do with the mysterious packages. Finally, halfway through the May entries, she gave up, closed the diary, and crawled into bed. Perhaps she would learn more in the morning before she had to go in and get started in the kitchen.

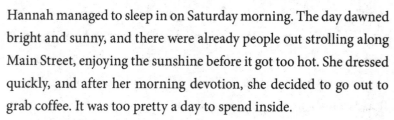

Hannah managed to sleep in on Saturday morning. The day dawned bright and sunny, and there were already people out strolling along Main Street, enjoying the sunshine before it got too hot. She dressed quickly, and after her morning devotion, she decided to go out to grab coffee. It was too pretty a day to spend inside.

She tucked a couple of the journals into her bag and headed out. Jump Start was only a few blocks away, and a few minutes later, she was seated at a table by the window, sipping an iced coffee as she perused Helen's account of her own life, from crushes to school to helping out with chores around the house.

Helen emerged as a person with strong opinions who knew what she wanted. She talked about how tired her dad was after long days in the mine, and how they worked hard to conserve fuel in the cold winter months when the house got so drafty. Her mother had some kind of chronic illness that flared up repeatedly, though Helen didn't specify what it was. By the time she'd made it to December 1953, Hannah understood a lot more about what it had been like to grow up in a mining town, but she was no closer to seeing a connection to the envelopes.

Hannah closed the first journal and looked around the small coffee shop, which was busy on this Saturday morning. Two women Hannah recognized from church sat at a table in the corner, talking over an open Bible. Marshall Fredericks, the local food critic who had given Hannah such great ideas for the Hot Spot in his initial review, pecked away at a laptop in the corner. He acknowledged her with a friendly nod, but was obviously focused on his work, so Hannah stayed put.

She took another sip of coffee and started the next journal. This one was from 1956, when Helen would have been eighteen. She had finished school and gotten a job cleaning the camp foreman's house. His home, she recorded, was many times the size of the houses the workers lived in. It had insulation from the heat and cold, polished wood floors, and an indoor privy. Helen saved as much as she could, though she did covet the pretty blue dress Loraine Bradshaw had worn to church on Sunday and thought she might splurge and buy herself a new dress.

By that point, Helen seemed to have been spending a lot of time with Walter Knicely too. He worked in the mine along with his father and older brother, and he hated it. He gave most of his paychecks to his parents to buy food for the family, but he managed to put some aside, and he and Helen were making plans. Plans for what, Helen didn't say, though Hannah—knowing that they had married and left Russell—suspected they had been saving for and plotting their escape. Whatever flirtation there had been with Bert Meisel, it was obviously over by then. There was no mention of him here. She supposed Lacy had the journal from 1955. Hopefully there would be something in it that would reveal more about Bert.

In this journal, there were several mentions of a cough her father couldn't shake, and more mentions of "Mama's spells." That made it sound like whatever was wrong with her wasn't so much a physical illness as a mental one. Or maybe Hannah was just reading with a modern eye and that wasn't what Helen meant at all. It was hard to know. There was an entry about an aunt on her father's side who had passed away, but not much else of consequence as far as Hannah could see.

And, of course, Hannah paid close attention to entries that mentioned Nancy. Nancy had gotten the highest marks in her year at school. Nancy had won a writing contest and got to go all the way to Louisville, and she was being insufferable about it. Nancy always left a mess behind her and never cleaned up her side of the room.

By the time Hannah had finished her iced coffee, she was halfway through the second diary. As much as she was enjoying this window into the life of young Helen, she had things to do, and she wasn't finding the answers she was after. She didn't know if they would ever find answers about what happened to Helen and Nancy, or whether it would get her any closer to understanding the contents of the envelopes, even if she did.

As she walked to her apartment, she decided that she couldn't sit around reading diaries any longer—or at least, not only that. She was ready to take action. As she walked, she pulled her phone out and called Lacy.

"Hey," Lacy said. "What's up?"

"Do you want to take a trip tomorrow?"

"Where?"

"Eastern Kentucky."

"Ooh. A big trip."

"I figure if we leave right after church, we could make it there and back before supper." Dad had invited her to eat with him and Uncle Gordon, and she didn't want to miss that.

"And what are you thinking we'll do while we're there?"

"We're going to talk to Madison. It's high time we find out what she knows."

Chapter Eighteen

Hannah stayed up far too late on Saturday night reading through another of Helen's diaries, but her perseverance was rewarded. She was about to give up and go to bed when she spotted something. On a second read-through, another piece of the puzzle fell into place.

She stopped Lacy on the way into church Sunday morning. "The handkerchiefs," Hannah said. "Nancy made them."

"What?" Lacy's eyes widened.

"I was reading your grandma's diary last night," Hannah said. "This was one from 1949, when she was eleven and Nancy was nine." She held out a diary, opened to a page halfway through, and found the entry for April 5. The writing was neat and precise, even more so than in the diaries as Helen got older.

She passed it to Lacy and read it again over her friend's shoulder.

> *I was trying to help Nancy with her stitching today, but she's impossible. I know she's just learning, and Mama says I need to be patient with her, but it's hard when she doesn't even seem to want to try.*
>
> *We were working on the handkerchiefs we're meant to make for Aunt Genevieve, and I only got partway through the*

W on one of mine while Nancy finished both of hers. The stitching is all uneven, and she even put the letters upside down! She was rushing so she could get back to her book, which is maddening. Mama says she's young and I must be patient with her. She's learning, and it's not my duty to correct her, but I don't see why Mama doesn't. She is becoming impossible!

"That's it," Hannah said. "Those are the handkerchiefs you guys have."

"Whoa," Lacy said. "They were embroidered by my great-aunt Nancy when she was a kid. That's such a great clue. Nice job finding this."

"It doesn't explain how they ended up in those packages or why the packages were delivered to you and your mom, unfortunately. But it does indicate a further connection to your grandmother and your great-aunt." The clues had started to point that way, but this was proof. "So now we just need to figure out what the handkerchiefs have to do with any of this."

"Maybe we'll find out today," Lacy said. "Maybe Madison will be able to tell us."

"Meet you right here after the service?" Hannah said.

Lacy nodded. "I can't wait."

"Are you sure your mom can't join us?"

"She wishes she could, but she says she promised Melba she'd take her shopping this afternoon."

"She's going to miss out on the fun."

Hannah was excited, but she managed to pay attention during the church service. Pastor Bob's sermon on forgiveness was particularly poignant, and they sang several of Hannah's favorite hymns. However, by the time she'd said hello to her dad and the rest of her family, she was ready to go. She found Lacy waiting in the shade of an eastern redbud tree near Hannah's car.

"I'm sorry," Hannah said. "I got away as quickly as I could."

"It's all right," Lacy said. "I'm sure it took some maneuvering to get away from Mitch Thomas."

"Thankfully, I didn't have to do that today." With everything else going on, she hadn't told Lacy about her conversation with Mitch at the Hot Spot. "Get in, and I'll tell you what happened."

As they headed for the highway, Hannah told Lacy about her honest conversation with Mitch and his respectful acceptance.

"That seems like a very mature way to handle it," Lacy said.

"Well, Liam was the one who suggested that the direct approach was the kindest," she said. "And I guess he was right."

"It sounds like he was," Lacy said, a smug smile on her face.

Hannah ignored the implication. She wasn't about to mess up her growing friendship with Liam because everyone else chose to read into it. Besides, Lacy was hardly one to talk. She hadn't dated in over a decade. She'd never had to deal with the abysmal world of dating apps or trying to find a good match when she was in her thirties. It was a wasteland, and one Hannah didn't have time for right now. Not everyone was lucky enough to find their person when they were still in college.

Changing the subject, Hannah asked, "How is the egg business going?"

Lacy told her about a new chicken breed she was hoping to expand into. "Araucana aren't the most practical bird, as there are other breeds that produce far more eggs in a year, but these hens lay eggs that are the most gorgeous pale blue color. I bet people would pay a premium for those, don't you?"

"Not when you're buying them in the quantities I am, but probably at a farmstand. Especially around Easter, when they'd make for an interesting egg-coloring background," Hannah said. "In LA, I used to pay a ridiculous sum at the local farmers market for a dozen eggs, but they were always such a gorgeous mix of tans and browns and blues that I didn't care. The eggs were good too, with nice dark yolks that tasted so much better than the supermarket ones. They weren't as good as yours, though."

"And mine don't cost an arm and a leg," Lacy said.

They talked more about the chickens as they drove, and then about business at Neil's store.

"Things are going so well that we've decided to start putting aside a little each month for renovations on the cottage," Lacy said. "It's a shame to have it sitting empty. We figure we can always rent it out, although the hope is that we can convince Mom to move in. She won't be able to do the stairs at her apartment forever, so we want to have the cottage ready whenever she gets tired of being so stubborn."

"I'm not sure it's stubbornness that's keeping her from moving home," Hannah reminded Lacy carefully. The last thing she wanted to do was get in the middle of family drama, but she'd love to help resolve it. "I get the impression that she doesn't want to impose."

"She wouldn't be imposing," Lacy said with an exasperated groan. "We've told her a dozen times we want her there. Why doesn't she believe it?"

"I think she wants to give you the chance to take ownership of the farm, to really feel like it's yours," Hannah said. "She might be worried that her presence will affect that."

"But I've told her so many times we want her. I don't know how to convince her I mean it."

"Maybe try again," Hannah said lamely. "Or maybe when you get that cottage fixed up, that will show her you're serious. That there's a place for her, and it's not right on top of you, so she could live on the property she loves most and still give you space. It really is the perfect solution."

Lacy was quiet for a moment, and then she finally said, "Maybe."

Hannah decided to let it go. She could make observations, but she couldn't make Lacy and Christine see that they both wanted the same thing unless they wanted to see it.

They talked about the restaurant for a while, and Lacy chatted about what she was going to serve at a dinner party the following night. As they drove, the landscape shifted, the hills and undulating fields of bluegrass changing slowly into the larger slopes of the Appalachian Mountains. The mountains rolled out, one after another, and the towns grew smaller and farther apart, but the scenery was breathtaking.

Finally, they left the main highway for a road that threaded around curves and past a river toward the town of Harlan, the seat of Harlan County. The GPS led them through the small town, a pretty little place hugged on two sides by steep green slopes.

They passed brick buildings, stone churches, and the stately courthouse with its neoclassical façade. They passed beautiful old homes and several restaurants Hannah wouldn't mind checking out. The law firm of Maris & Maris had an office here somewhere, but they didn't think it likely Brian would be there on a Sunday.

Instead, they followed a road leading out of the main downtown area and up a hill. After a few miles, they parked in front of the Victorian home Hannah had seen online. The mansard roof and the cupola were beautiful, but now that she saw it in person, it felt a bit incongruous to have a Victorian mansion set up in the hills outside an old mining town.

But as they stepped out of the car, she saw that the house overlooked the town and the rows of saw-toothed mountains beyond, and she understood why it had been built right here. The view was unparalleled.

"This is a lovely house," Hannah said. "Obviously whoever built it had money and wanted to make sure everyone knew it."

"They weren't working in a coal mine—that's for sure."

"No, they probably weren't. Owned the mine, maybe."

As they walked past a silver BMW and a white Toyota on their way to the door, Lacy asked, "Do you have a plan for what we'll say?"

"Not really," Hannah said. "I was thinking I would ask for Madison and see what happens."

A dog barked from somewhere inside the house. They stepped up onto the wraparound porch, which featured half a dozen chairs for taking in the view, and rang the doorbell.

A moment later, a woman opened the door, holding the collar of a very excited golden retriever.

"Hello?" She looked at them questioningly. Hannah recognized her as Danielle, the woman behind the website Christine had found.

Through the open doorway, Hannah noticed the pale walls hung with heavy-framed pictures that she'd seen online.

"Hello. We were hoping to talk to Madison," Hannah said.

"Madison's not here right now," Danielle replied. "She's meeting some friends out at the lake. Is there something I can help you with?"

Was there? Hannah didn't know what to ask. She wanted to demand answers, to find out how this family was connected to Lacy's, but she couldn't figure out how to say that. After all, Danielle might not know anything about it.

"Maybe," Lacy said. "Do you have any connection to Russell, Kentucky?"

"I don't believe so." Danielle released the dog's collar, and he poked his nose out to sniff them. "Didn't that place shut down decades ago?"

"It did," Lacy confirmed. "How about Blackberry Valley? Do you know of it?"

"Never heard of it. Though it sounds lovely."

"It is," Lacy said. "What about Helen or Nancy Whitmore? Have you heard of them?"

"I'm afraid not," she said.

"You're not related to them in any way? Through your husband's family somehow?"

"If so, it's far enough back that I've never heard those names," she said. "What does all of this have to do with Madison?"

Hannah didn't know how to answer. Should she tell the truth? How would they even begin to explain?

"Thank you so much for your help," Lacy said, turning to go. "We appreciate it."

Too surprised to argue, Hannah followed her friend to the car. It wasn't until they were inside that she found her voice. "What was that?"

"She didn't know anything," Lacy replied.

"You don't think she was deflecting?" Hannah secretly agreed with Lacy but wanted to make sure.

Danielle still stood in the open doorway, watching them.

"I don't," Lacy replied. "I think she meant it when she said she'd never heard of Blackberry Valley or Nancy and Helen, and was genuinely confused as to why we were asking."

"I think you're right." Hannah put the car in gear and they started down the hill. "But now I'm even more confused."

"We'll go find Madison," Lacy said, tapping at her phone screen. "She's the key to all this."

"How will we do that?"

"Her mom said she was at the lake," Lacy reminded her. "And it turns out there's a lake outside of town that, according to the town's website, 'is popular for swimming, boating, and recreation.'"

"The recreation part seems a bit extraneous," Hannah said. "Given that swimming and boating are recreational activities."

"Hey, I didn't write the website. I just read it," Lacy said. "It's a five-minute drive from here."

"Let's go."

They found the lake easily enough, and the parking lot was crowded on this hot summer day. Beyond the lot, there was a beach packed with chairs and umbrellas, and a dock and a boat launch to the right, by the bathrooms and snack bar.

"How in the world are we going to find her?" Hannah wondered aloud, scanning the crowd. There had to be hundreds of people there. "And what if she doesn't want to talk to us after we tracked her down like this? I don't know if I would."

"I think we just start searching," Lacy said, shrugging. "She's an adult. We're two nice church ladies who want to ask her some questions in a public space. She's met you before. If we find her, she'll either talk to us, or she won't. Either way, we're no worse off than we are now."

Hannah felt ridiculously out of place in her church dress at the beach, where nearly everyone else was in swimsuits or shorts and flip-flops. She was not looking forward to walking up and down the beach searching for Madison.

Fortunately, they didn't have to. Hannah spotted her halfway across the parking lot. She recognized Madison immediately—the blond hair, the big, expressive eyes. She wore denim shorts, flip-flops, and a tank top over her swimsuit, and she was hoisting a beach chair from the bed of a pickup truck. A guy in a swimsuit and T-shirt stood in the truck bed, trying to wrestle an inflatable flamingo out of the truck.

"Madison?" Hannah called.

Madison glanced around. Hannah waved, and she saw the moment Madison recognized her. The younger woman froze, and her expression went from confusion to panic. She stared from Hannah to Lacy and back again.

"Hi," Hannah said. "I'm Hannah. We met at the Hot Spot, in Blackberry Valley."

"And I'm Lacy." Lacy held out her hand.

"I know," Madison said, not shaking Lacy's hand.

That was interesting. Madison hadn't met Lacy while she was in town.

"We've been looking for you," Hannah said. "I was hoping we could ask you some questions about the packages you dropped off while you were in town."

For a moment, Madison didn't say anything. She opened her mouth and shut it again. Then she blurted, "I can't talk to you." She spun on her heel and fled to the beach.

Chapter Nineteen

Hannah instinctively started to follow Madison, but Lacy grabbed her arm. "What are you doing?" her friend whispered.

"I don't know," Hannah replied, shocked at herself. They weren't police officers apprehending a suspect. They had no real right to follow someone who clearly didn't want to talk to them. She could only imagine what people would have thought about two women in church clothes chasing a younger woman into the lake. Not to mention how much more terrified Madison would have been, and how less likely to talk to them.

The whole way back to Blackberry Valley, Lacy and Hannah discussed why Madison might have fled, but they couldn't come up with an answer that made sense.

"Maybe she found the keys somewhere, like at a garage sale or antique store, traced the descendants of people who grew up in the mining town, and decided to return them?" Hannah suggested, though it sounded unlikely even as she said it.

"Why would she do that?" Lacy asked. "And why not include a note explaining what it was all about? And what about the handkerchiefs my great-aunt embroidered?"

Those theories didn't add up, and neither did anything else they came up with.

"Maybe she was paid to deliver the packages," Lacy suggested.

"But who paid her? And why Madison specifically?"

"I don't know. Perhaps she's a descendent of the people who owned the mine back in the day. You saw that house she lives in. We both thought that could have been an owner's house," Lacy said. "Maybe she wants to apologize for how horrible it was and make it right. That could be a reason for her to find the descendants of the people who worked there and—"

"Send them random things with no material value or explanation, to drive them crazy?"

"That's maybe a bit harsh," Lacy said. "But fair enough."

"What we're missing is the connection to your grandmother and her sister. They're directly tied to all this. The handkerchiefs prove that," Hannah said. "Your family tree doesn't connect with hers. And Danielle doesn't know who you or your mom are."

"She could have been lying," Lacy said.

"It didn't seem like she was. You said earlier you believed her."

"Well, now I'm getting desperate and willing to consider any possibility. We don't know her. She could be an experienced liar. She could lie all day every day, and so she shows no signs of stress when she does it now."

"Okay, fine, that's a possibility, however remote," Hannah said. "But let's also keep on the table the possibility that she might have been telling the truth. She told us—two complete strangers who randomly showed up at her door—where her daughter was hanging out. If she was lying to us about anything else, surely she would have lied about that as well."

Lacy folded her arms across her chest. "So Danielle might not have known who we are or about my family, but Madison sure did."

"Absolutely. She recognized not only me, but also you, and she didn't even meet you while she was in Blackberry Valley," Hannah said.

"Which is kind of creepy, honestly."

"No creepier than us tracking her down at her home and then following her to the lake," Hannah pointed out. "The point is that she was obviously more than a simple messenger, paid to deliver the envelopes. She is involved with this somehow."

"But I can't figure out how," Lacy said.

They were no closer to the answer when they made it home to Blackberry Valley. If she hurried, Hannah would have enough time to throw together a salad and race to Dad's house for dinner.

"See you at puzzle night tomorrow?" Lacy asked as she climbed out of the car.

"I'll be there," Hannah promised.

"See you then," Lacy said, waving. "Thank you for a fun day."

Hannah realized it had been a fun day. They may not have gotten the answers they were hoping for, but she'd had time with her best friend, and she'd gotten to see a place she hadn't been to before. She couldn't complain about that.

They'd just have to keep looking.

After a lively dinner, full of good food and hilarious stories from Dad's and Uncle Gordon's childhood, Hannah headed home.

She was exhausted, surprised as ever by how tiring driving could be when it mostly involved sitting. At home, she took a shower and climbed into bed, where she fell asleep quickly and slept deeply.

When she woke Monday morning, the sky was a pale blue, and sunlight cascaded over the redbrick building across the street, casting it in a gorgeous golden glow.

She made coffee and read her Bible, and then she returned to the diaries. She had a lot to do today. She needed to tackle laundry and get groceries, and she had an appointment to talk to an organic sheep farmer Amos Bowers had recommended. She also wanted to dig through the diaries for anything that would help her connect Helen and Nancy to Madison. She flipped open a few covers, looking for some of the books that recorded later years. She was guessing—and it was truly a guess—that they might contain more pertinent information.

The latest journals she had were from 1958, 1960, and 1962, when Helen would have been in her early twenties. Hannah decided to start with the earliest year, so she opened the cover and started reading.

Even in her busy young adulthood, Helen remained a faithful journaler, recording bits and pieces of her thoughts most days. Many of the journal entries didn't touch on big topics, but rather recorded the daily interactions of life in the mining town. Helen continued to clean the house belonging to the mine's foreman. She found the man's wife overly picky and difficult to deal with, but the work easy enough, and the foreman was kind whenever she ran into him.

Hannah read about Helen's upcoming wedding to Walter, and wondered whether she had missed a proposal of some sort in an earlier journal or one of the ones Lacy had, or whether they had simply decided to get married. Helen seemed practical enough that Hannah doubted a fanciful proposal and dramatic declaration of love would have been her cup of tea. Hannah wasn't sure big dramatic proposals were even a thing at that time—perhaps they were more of a modern invention. In any case, the ceremony was set for early May, a simple service in the chapel followed by cake and punch, according to Helen's notes. Nancy would be her maid of honor and was helping to make the paper flowers that would decorate the church pews.

What about Bert? What had their romance been like? Hannah didn't know, because he wasn't mentioned here. That made sense, since his letters had stopped well before the time she was reading about, but she still wanted to track down what had happened there if she could. But that wasn't her focus right now.

As the wedding day grew closer, the entries were filled with notes about nonstop preparations, and then there were a few days of entries missing when the big day arrived. When she resumed writing, Helen noted that the service had been beautiful, the reception afterward a dream. Then they spent the rest of the day moving their things into the house they had rented in Russell, down the road from her new husband's parents' home. The new house was smaller than the ones they were used to, and it was in shabby condition, but it was theirs together, so it was a dream come true. It was perfect for a young couple just starting out.

Walter worked in the mine, and she still worked for the foreman, even though some people in town thought she should stop now that she was a married woman. But she refused, because they were saving their pennies. They had one goal—to get out of Russell as quickly as possible.

Close to the end of the year, Helen recorded symptoms that made her suspect there might be a child on the way, though she would need to wait and see to be sure. Hannah couldn't imagine having to wait for news like that. Nowadays a woman could take a simple test at home and find out within minutes, but those hadn't existed then. A visit to the doctor might have removed any question, but it didn't sound like they had money for such things. The diary ended without an answer, though Hannah did the math in her head and realized Helen had likely been pregnant with Christine when she wrote the entry.

It had been a big year for Helen. Nancy hadn't been mentioned much, especially after the wedding. She was still living at home with their parents when Helen moved out, as far as Hannah could tell. If there had been some tension or disagreement between the sisters, it wasn't mentioned in the pages of the diary.

What was mentioned several times was that her father's persistent cough had not gone away.

Dad's cough has gotten worse, Helen wrote in February. *The cold surely isn't helping. He says he'll be better when spring comes again, although we all know it's probably not true. It didn't get better last year when the snow melted.*

And again, in June, she wrote, *Nancy says Dad has cut back his hours in the mine. He can't keep it up with his lungs the way they are. At least now he can afford to do that, since he doesn't have to worry about my care any longer.*

There were also several mentions of Mama's "spells."

Mama had another one of her spells. Last time she was in bed for a week. I hope it's not that long this time. I went over and helped cook, but I can't do that every night. I'm too exhausted. I just feel like I can't sleep enough, no matter how much I rest.

Hannah eyed the other journal, the one from 1962. Wouldn't that have been just after Helen, Walter, and young Christine had moved from Russell to Lexington? She thought so, and hoped that the journal might contain the clues she was searching for. But she needed to get going. She had to meet the sheep farmer in half an hour, and she would need to hurry to make it on time.

By late afternoon, Hannah had toured the sheep farm and signed a contract to buy a significant portion of the restaurant's lamb and sheep's milk products, such as feta cheese, from him. She'd also made a trip to Blackberry Market to refill her fridge and had even washed not only her clothes but also her sheets and towels. The whole apartment smelled clean and fresh as she set out the ingredients to make a blackberry crumble for Lacy's puzzle night. Cobbler was delicious, but it was also forgiving and not an exact science, which left her mind free to mull over her next step in the mystery.

They had to find a link between Nancy, Helen, and Madison, and they weren't going to get it from Madison herself. Yesterday's interaction had made that clear. Hannah was doing all she could to learn about Helen and Nancy and how their relationship had fallen apart, but she was still missing the connection to Madison. Which meant she needed to find out more about Madison, with or without her help.

As Hannah worked, mixing flour, sugar, oats, and butter to make the crumble topping, she racked her brain, trying to come up with any detail she'd missed that would help her find the missing pieces. Was there something about Madison's appearance in the security footage of her delivering the envelope to Christine's mail slot that might provide a clue? Hannah didn't see how. But she didn't have any better ideas, so she called up the footage and set it to play.

This was probably a waste of time. She'd already seen this footage how many times? But she watched it again, just in case, keeping an eye out for anything—anything at all—that might tell her something she didn't know about Madison.

And this time, she noticed something she hadn't before.

Chapter Twenty

Hannah watched the footage again, pausing the video when she had the best view of the tote bag slung over Madison's shoulder. There was writing on the bag. How had she not seen this before? Well, to be fair, it was probably because she could only see a few letters on the bag, and they didn't tell her very much.

M-A... That was all she could make out from the top line of text. The folds of the bag obscured whatever else was printed there.

Below it was another line of text. The way the bag hung and the fabric lay, she could see an *M* at the beginning of that word, and an *S* at the end of it.

M-A

M...S

The bag itself was a rich hunter green, with a lighter green swirl radiating from the center.

That wasn't a lot to go on. But maybe it was better than nothing.

It might simply spell out Madison's full name, perhaps as a monogrammed gift from someone. Or it might be a company name. Hannah was always carrying free, branded tote bags from one event or another. It couldn't hurt to try to figure out what it meant.

Hannah suddenly planned to solve a different kind of puzzle that night.

When Hannah arrived at Lacy's house for puzzle night, she saw that her friend had set up folding card tables, each with a jigsaw puzzle, and several chairs. According to the pictures on the boxes, one was a puzzle of adorable puppies, one was a beach scene, and one was a colored gradient, going from a red to pink and purple and then to shades of blue. That one looked the hardest.

"Hey! Come on in," Lacy said, ushering her inside. "Welcome. And thank you for this." She took the cobbler from Hannah's hands. "Feel free to take a seat at any of the tables and get to work."

Hannah glanced around the room. Christine was bent over the puppies, while Vera, from their church group, was bravely starting on the color gradient. Latricia and Marty, who they'd gone to high school with, wandered around with Francine Bagby and Lacy's neighbor Anna, looking at the puzzle boxes.

"Thank you," Hannah said. "But I sort of brought my own puzzle to work on today."

"Oh yeah?" Lacy tilted her head. "What's that?"

Hannah put her backpack on the kitchen table. "I'm trying to figure out where a bag is from."

Hannah had started making guesses about phrases that fit underneath the letters on Madison's tote. *Making Memories. Mark Morris. Map Milestones.* She knew this was probably a hopeless task, but she wouldn't be able to focus on jigsaw puzzles with this on her mind. She had to at least try to sort it out.

"It's from that security camera footage," she explained. Suspecting the video itself might be in demand, Hannah had brought her laptop, so she set it up and opened the video. Several of the ladies crowded around the small screen, and Hannah hit play.

"What is this?" Anna asked, squinting at the screen. Her graying hair hung over her shoulders.

"Where is that camera?" Latricia asked.

"It's outside the stationery store on Main Street," Lacy said. On screen, Madison had just come into view.

"I didn't know there was a camera there," Vera said.

"It's a shame that business owners have to go to such lengths to protect their livelihoods," Marty said, shaking her head.

When the best view of the bag came onto the screen, Hannah paused the footage. "There. That's what I'm trying to figure out."

"Who is that girl?" Vera asked.

"That's not the point," Lacy said. "It's her bag we're interested in."

Christine left the puppy puzzle to stare at the screen. "That's Madison?" she asked, pointing at the computer.

"That's right. This is that security footage." Hannah realized Christine probably hadn't seen it before. "That's your door."

"It is indeed." She squinted at the screen.

Several of the other women exclaimed over this fact, asking why they were looking at Christine's door and what this was all about.

"Oh, this is easy," Christine said.

"It is?" Hannah glanced at Lacy, who appeared as surprised as Hannah was.

"Sure," she said. "It says Maris and Maris."

Hannah smacked herself on the forehead. Christine was right. "The law firm."

"The one her dad works at," Christine agreed. "So maybe we need to figure out whether there's a reason she's advertising her father's law firm."

It was probably nothing. Hannah herself had lots of tote bags from different places, and most of them were kind of random. When she carried a branded tote bag, it didn't mean anything except that the bag was useful. She had one from the British Library she'd picked up on a trip to London two years before. It didn't mean she had any real connection to the British Library, except that she'd appreciated seeing the Jane Austen manuscript, Beatles lyrics, and the original Magna Carta on display. The tote bag she'd left with merely proved that she'd been to the gift shop, not that she was anxious to advertise for the British Library.

But she was desperate for any clue at this point, so when the others returned to their jigsaw puzzles, Hannah stayed at her laptop. She navigated to the law firm's page and poked around for well, anything that pointed to Madison besides the obvious family connection. There was the page that listed the two Marises in question, Brian and his brother, Craig. There were photos of them with bios listing their resumes, from where they'd gotten their degrees to the kinds of law they had experience with. There was a page of contact information where the public could send them an email. And there was the main page, which discussed the legal services offered: family law, estates and wills, real estate, contracts, and tax law.

An idea started to form in Hannah's mind. "Did your mother have a will?" Hannah asked Christine.

Christine frowned in confusion. "Yes. Both of my parents did. They had it drawn up by a lawyer in Lexington. They didn't have much, but when they were both gone, I sold their house and their few assets. The money went right into the farm."

"What about your aunt Nancy? She died late last year, right?"

"Yes, but I have no idea if she had a will," Christine said. "Like I said, I never knew her."

"But if she had one, she could have used that law firm," Lacy said, pointing at the screen.

"She could have," Christine said. "But even if she had, she wouldn't leave me anything."

"And even if she did leave you something, why would it be a couple of keys and a cryptic poem?" Lacy said. "Unless she was totally twisted, and this was her idea of a joke." Lacy had pulled out her own laptop and was running a search of her own.

"Even if that's the case, that's not how estates are distributed," Christine said. "You get an official notification from the executor, not an unmarked envelope shoved through your mail slot. When my mom passed, I was the executor, and it took so much time and effort to get the estate settled. You have to file with the probate court, notify all the people named in the will, and place a notice in the paper for creditors. It's not like on TV shows, where there's a dramatic will reading that changes everything."

Hannah's dad had handled all of that business when Mom passed, so Hannah wasn't very familiar with the process.

"Besides, we went to his house and asked his wife, Danielle, if she knew Nancy Whitmore, but she didn't," Lacy said. She paused, her fingers frozen in midair over the keyboard. "But why would she, now that I think about it?"

"Danielle doesn't work for the law firm," Christine added, giving Lacy a look that indicated they would discuss the issue later. "Just the brothers."

"So if Brian doesn't talk about his work at home, it's entirely plausible his wife would never have heard the name from the will."

"But that still doesn't solve the problem that this isn't how estates are distributed," Christine said. "The executor contacts the people named in the will directly, at least in my experience."

"What if there is no executor?" Hannah asked.

There was a moment of silence while Christine processed the question. "There must be one."

"What if the person who dies has no family?" Hannah insisted.

"Then they would name a friend, I suppose," Christine said. "Or perhaps the lawyer who drew it up. I'm not sure. I had a friend who served as a court-appointed administrator when someone passed without naming one for their will." She tilted her head to one side. "Why? Do you think my aunt...?"

Hannah was thankful that, aside from Christine and Lacy, everyone else seemed to be focused on their jigsaw puzzles.

"I don't know." But Hannah was already navigating to the *Harlan County Times* website. "You said a notice needs to be placed in the local paper, right?"

Christine nodded. "At least it did when Mom passed. It's to let any unknown creditors know to make a claim before the estate is settled."

"An announcement in the newspaper?" Lacy said. "That feels kind of outdated."

Christine shrugged. "I don't disagree with you. I'm just telling you what I had to do."

Hannah clicked on the search bar for the *Harlan County Times* and typed in the name *Nancy Whitmore*. Would a legal announcement come up in a search, even if it did exist? But as she scanned the header of the website, she saw that LEGALS was one of the tabs she could click on, along with NEWS, SPORTS, LIFESTYLE, OPINION, OBITUARIES, and CLASSIFIEDS. She clicked on the LEGALS tab, and searched for the name *Nancy* on the page.

The announcement came up immediately.

NOTICE TO CREDITORS: ESTATE OF Nancy F. Whitmore. The Hon. Carolanne Rowley, Judge of the Court of Probate, District of Harlan Probate Court, by decree ordered that all claims must be presented to the fiduciary at the address below. Failure to promptly present any such claim may result in the loss of rights to recover on such claim. Michelle R. Gowan, Chief Clerk. The fiduciary is: Brian Maris, Maris and Maris, 324 S. 1st Street, Harlan, KY 40831.

"Does this mean Brian was Nancy's executor?" Hannah asked, pointing at the screen.

"I think it probably does," Christine said. "I'm obviously not a lawyer, so I don't know for sure, but when I had to do this for Mom, it was my name there on that line."

"Okay," Hannah said. "If Maris and Maris handled Nancy's estate, then is there any chance Madison was working for them when she came to Blackberry Valley?"

"There is a very good chance of that," Lacy said, looking up from her laptop. "She posted a new video on her social media page. Check it out."

"I thought her social media was all videos of book reviews." Hannah leaned over to see.

"It is," Lacy said. "But look. Madison just posted this video last night." She clicked on the first recording in the lineup.

"Hi guys, I'm back with another review," Madison said into the camera. "This one is pretty different from the kind of book I normally review, but it's a good one. You see, this summer, I'm working for my dad and my uncle in their law firm, and it's kinda boring, if I'm honest. Filing, data entry—that kind of thing. But occasionally I get to do something fun. Like last weekend I got to drive over to a pretty small town on an errand for one of the clients' estates, and I got to eat good food and drink good coffee—all paid for by the firm, I might add."

"Not a bad gig for a recent college grad," Hannah observed.

Madison went on. "But for the most part, I'm just typing away at a computer, bored to tears. I figured since I was working at a law firm, I might as well read some books about being a lawyer." She held up a copy of John Grisham's *The Firm*. "I found this vintage book, and oh my goodness, you guys, it's so good. Don't let the fact that it's the kind of book my dad would read scare you away. From the first page, you're totally drawn into this world of high-stakes legal drama, and—"

Lacy muted the video. "I assume it goes on to discuss the book from there, but that's what we needed to know, right? That's the connection to Aunt Nancy. Madison works for the law firm that handled her estate."

"So Aunt Nancy sent the packages?" Christine asked.

"It does seem like maybe she directed her lawyer to have the packages sent to us after her death," Lacy said.

"But why?" Hannah chimed in. "Why the envelopes and not an official letter from the law firm? Why did she want you to have those things? What message was she trying to send?"

"And why not send the message a little more clearly?" Lacy said. "Maybe it should have started with, 'Hi, I'm the aunt you've never met. Here's why I sent these things to you.' Not some random bits and a cryptic poem."

On its surface, Hannah agreed with Lacy's sentiment. But she also knew that the method used must have made sense to Aunt Nancy somehow. People usually acted in ways that felt rational to them, even if they didn't make sense to anyone else. "There has to be some logic to Nancy's choices, at least in her mind," Hannah said. "We need to see things through her eyes."

"Which would be a lot easier if she were still alive, or if I'd ever known her," Christine said.

"Or if we knew anything about the way she thought," Lacy added.

"If she was so anxious to get in touch, why didn't she do it while she was alive?" Christine said.

Hannah couldn't disagree that there were still open questions. But they were getting close to solving the mystery—she could feel it. They just needed to continue digging.

"We should keep reading those journals," Hannah said. "If there's any way to understand Nancy's thinking or more about what happened, it's through them."

Christine and Lacy wore matching doubtful expressions, look-ing so much like mother and daughter that Hannah nearly laughed out loud.

"I have a better idea," Christine said. "Why don't we go to Harlan and demand that Brian Maris tell us what's going on?"

That was an option too. Hannah couldn't deny it would proba-bly be more effective at getting the answers they wanted, than read-ing the old journals. Lacy nodded, apparently agreeing with her mother.

"All right," Hannah said. "When do we go back to eastern Kentucky?"

Chapter Twenty-One

I t wasn't as hard to arrange a night off from the restaurant as Hannah thought it might be. Her staff assured her that they could handle business without her on Wednesday.

Hannah was still hesitant, but Elaine reminded her that Wednesdays were not their busiest days, and they had her phone number if any issues arose. Maybe Hannah should have waited until the following Monday, when she already had the day off, but she, Christine, and Lacy all refused to wait a full week to get answers. Besides, there was never truly a day off in the restaurant business, so she had to make one. She confirmed with Christine and Lacy that they were good to go on Wednesday.

Hannah spent Tuesday morning reading through Helen's diaries, hunting for more information about what had happened between her and Nancy, but nothing in the diaries explained their falling out. There was one entry in 1960—Christine was a baby, and Hannah didn't have the journal that recorded her birth—where Helen referred to tension between herself and her sister.

Nancy stopped by today for what I thought would be a nice visit, but it was really to say that I needed to help at home more, now that Daddy is so poorly and I'm no longer working. What does she think I'm doing—just sitting around here twiddling my thumbs? I'm exhausted and never get a moment to myself, and most days I feel like it's all I can do to keep Christine and Walter fed and clothed.

Of course I want to help Mama and Daddy. I do feel bad that Nancy has so much to do, but it's not like her job at the phone company takes up much time. I try to remember that she doesn't understand, and that someday, when she has a baby of her own, she'll see.

But that was it, at least from the journals in Hannah's possession. Maybe they would never know what had happened.

The restaurant was busy Tuesday night, causing Hannah to second guess whether it would be a good idea to leave it all behind on Wednesday. Elaine must have seen her looking anxious, because she said, "We've got this, boss. We're a well-oiled machine at this point."

Hannah smiled gratefully. Her hostess was right. They would be okay without her for one night.

On Wednesday, Hannah packed snacks and made sandwiches and filled a travel mug with coffee. Then she waited for Lacy and Christine to pick her up.

"Hannah, I found it!" Lacy exclaimed as Hannah climbed into the car.

"You found what?" Hannah asked, clicking her seat belt into place.

"This is Helen's journal from 1961." Lacy took a black leather volume out of her bag and held it up. She had inserted half a dozen brightly-colored sticky notes on the pages. "I don't know how I over-looked this one before. That's the year my grandparents and my mom moved out of Russell."

"What does your grandmother say?" Hannah asked. She reached over the seat and took the journal.

"There are a bunch of passages about it. Just go to the first sticky note."

Hannah flipped to the first page Lacy had marked. "Okay, this is from March 3."

> We've finally saved up enough, and Walter gave notice at the mine today. He was told we would need to be out of the house in two weeks. It can't come soon enough. We have so much to do, but I cannot wait to be out of this place.
>
> We haven't told our families yet. Walter's parents will be happy for us. All they've ever wanted was for Walter to have a better life, and getting out of here is the only way that's going to happen. They'll know that.
>
> Mama will be sad that she won't get to see Christine as much, and Daddy will be sad too but will understand. He doesn't want Walter or anyone to have trouble with their lungs the way he does.
>
> But Nancy won't be supportive—not because she's sad, but because she will only be thinking about the work of caring for our parents and how it's all going to fall on her. I'm sorry about that—I truly am—but I can't stick around because of

it. There's no way I'm letting my daughter grow up in this horrible place.

I wish we could afford to move them with us, but we can't stay and continue to save. It would take years. Every day in those mines puts Walter in danger. Every day in this town, the very air poisons my daughter's lungs. Enough is enough.

"Wow," Christine said, her voice thick with emotion. "I mean, I guess I knew they probably left so I'd have a better life than they did growing up, but hearing it straight from her like that..." She let her voice trail off, and though her face was turned toward knee-high cornstalks flashing past the window, Hannah got the sense that her eyes had filled with tears.

"There was a passage in one of the journals I read from the year before, where Nancy asked her to help out more with caring for her parents, but Helen said she couldn't," Hannah said. "It sounds like maybe that was a point of tension that continued to build."

"What was wrong with him, Mom?" Lacy asked. "Your grandfather?"

"I always heard it was black lung," Christine said. "I don't know what that is, if I'm totally honest, but I guess it was pretty common among miners. Some kind of lung disease caused by breathing in coal dust."

"Hang on." Hannah looked it up on her phone, and a moment later, she read, "'Coal worker's pneumoconiosis, commonly referred to as black lung disease, occurs when coal dust is inhaled over time, leading to scarring in the lungs and impairing the ability to breathe.'"

"It sounds terrible," Lacy murmured. "He was sick with that, Great-Grandma was caring for him, and Nancy was helping."

"Yes, but Nancy's mother had her own health issue," Hannah said. "Her 'spells,' whatever those were. So she wasn't always able to care for her husband. Nancy had a job at the phone company, but she was caring for her parents too, and it was too much for her. Based on this journal entry, that was still a point of contention between the sisters."

"It doesn't get better," Lacy said. "Read the next passage from two days later."

Hannah flipped to the next sticky note.

I told Mama we were leaving today, and she cried but said she was happy for me. She made me promise to come back to visit and to take good care of Christine. Nancy didn't say anything. She just left the room. I know she's upset, but what am I supposed to do? Does she really think I'm going to stick around here because she doesn't want to wash all the laundry herself?

"Wow. She could have been a bit more sensitive," Christine said. "I'm sure it wasn't all about laundry for Nancy."

"True, but Helen was writing in her diary," Hannah said. "She never expected anyone but her to read it, so she was being honest about how she felt. And I imagine she was defensive about the hard call she had to make."

"Fair enough," Christine said.

"There's more," Lacy said. "Go to the next one, a few days later."

Once again, Hannah flipped through the pages and read the passage.

> *Nancy came by today and begged me not to leave. When I told her it was done and there was no turning back, she said I was being selfish and I would regret it. She said it's not fair for me to go off and leave her to care for Mama and Daddy alone. She also said all kinds of other things she must have thought would change my mind, but of course they didn't. They're not worth writing down here, as I have no desire to remember them. I told her I regret that more work will fall to her—I really am sorry about that—but I will get my daughter out of this town if it's the last thing I do.*

"I can honestly see both sides," Lacy said. "I can see why Grandma needed to get out, but I also understand why Nancy was upset. Caring for sick parents can't have been easy for Nancy to handle all on her own, especially if she had a job too."

"It sounds like Nancy didn't realize that a mother will do anything for her child," Christine said quietly. "I'm not surprised that Mom wouldn't be deterred. Any mother out there would understand that you do whatever it takes to give your child the best life you can. Even if it goes against what you want personally, you'll make the sacrifice for your child."

Hannah suddenly had the sense that Christine was talking about more than the decision her parents had made to leave Russell. She quietly flipped to the next marked page in the journal.

"The next part is where they actually leave," Lacy said. "And it sheds a different light on things."

We said goodbye today, and it was harder than I expected. Mama and Daddy cried, but it was Nancy that really got to me.

"Please don't leave me here," Nancy said, tears in her eyes. "I can't stay trapped in this awful town. If you do, I'll never speak to you again."

She can't mean that. I'll give her time to calm down, and she can reach out to me when she's ready. We're sisters after all.

"So their estrangement was about more than laundry," Hannah said.

"Of course it was," Christine said. "If Helen's leaving was enough to tear the sisters apart for the rest of their lives, it must have been about something much deeper than chores. The chores were simply something they could discuss when they couldn't verbalize what they were truly feeling. Nancy knew that if Mom left, she would be stuck in Russell, caring for her parents."

"*She* couldn't leave, not without abandoning her sick parents altogether," Lacy said, picking up the thread. "So Helen's leaving meant she was stuck. That's what Nancy was upset about."

"That Helen's choice meant Nancy didn't have one," Hannah said. "It makes sense."

"And Nancy never did abandon her parents, right?" Lacy asked. "When the mines closed a few years later, she must have moved with them to the new house. She cared for them until the end, didn't she?"

"It seems likely, since we know she never married or had kids. She never got to pursue the life she might have wanted for herself," Hannah said. "I wonder how much of that was by choice, and how much was by necessity."

"Surely she could have married if she'd wanted to," Lacy said.

"If she was a full-time caregiver, which it sounds like she must have been toward the end?" Christine shook her head. "Nancy would have had to find someone who was willing to move into her parents' home and organize their life around her sick folks. Perhaps she could have found someone who was willing to do that for love, but it sounds like she didn't."

"But her parents didn't live forever. What about after they passed away?"

"Her mother passed in 1972," Christine said. "Nancy would have been thirty-one. Which is certainly not too old these days." She looked pointedly at Hannah.

"What about thirty-five?" Hannah laughed.

"You're a spring chicken by today's standards. But at that time, it would have been quite old to be unmarried."

"So what we're saying is that the reason Nancy was so upset when Helen left was that it meant Nancy probably wouldn't be able to live the life she wanted," Lacy said.

"I don't know that Nancy could have known at the time that it would mean she wouldn't ever get married or anything like that," Hannah said. "But surely she could see that if Helen left, it meant that Nancy never could."

"And Nancy never forgave her for it," Lacy said.

"That's what it sounds like to me," Christine said.

"Even so, I can't imagine never talking to my brother again," Hannah said. "Just cutting him off entirely, never seeing his wife or kids again. It would be torture. I don't understand how anyone could do that."

"Hurt feelings have a way of festering if they're not addressed," Christine said. "Unless we find more detail in the journals, I suppose we'll never know exactly when and how they lost touch. Maybe it happened right away, with one dramatic conversation, or maybe it took years for them to drift apart entirely. But it sounds like we've probably found the root of the problem."

"Hang on. There's one entry where Helen talks about it," Lacy said.

Hannah flipped to the last tabbed page. "Here's what she says. It's a month later."

I got a letter back from Nancy today. I wrote her a letter soon after we got to Lexington to give her our address and explain again why we had to leave. She wrote to tell me again how selfish I am and that she doesn't know if she can ever forgive me. I don't know how to make her see that it isn't selfishness but love that made me leave. I love Christine too much to stay, and if she considers that selfish, then I guess we'll never see eye to eye on this. I do hope she will come around, but with how Nancy digs in her heels, I don't know.

"It's so sad," Christine said.

"They both wanted the same thing—a chance for a better life—but they didn't realize it because each of them could only see her own perspective," Lacy said. "If they had been able to talk it out, maybe they could have come to some compromise. Like, maybe Helen could have come back to help out on a regular schedule so Nancy would have had a break sometimes. I don't know. But there had to be a better way to resolve this than cutting each other out of their lives. If they already felt overwhelmed, I don't see how narrowing their support systems would have improved that."

"I'm sure they could have come up with a solution they were both happy with," Christine said.

Hannah ducked her head so neither of them could see her smile. It seemed that there was more than one generation of this family who talked around what they really felt by discussing something else. Hannah felt confident that, having opened that door, these two could work something out to solve both their problems. It was too late for Helen and Nancy, but it wasn't too late for Christine and Lacy.

"Did you read anything about Bert?" Hannah asked.

"Oh, yes, I found that diary too. Helen fell for him, but then he moved on, and eventually she did too."

"That's it?" Hannah was almost disappointed.

"I mean, there were a lot of tears and entries about how heartbroken she was. But then Walter took her back, and she realized he was the kind of man who would stick by her side. The kind of man she could trust. Things moved pretty quickly with them after that."

The three women finally reached the law firm of Maris & Maris. It was a brick two-story building on a side street off the main thoroughfare in town. There was a small lot behind the building, so they parked in there.

"Are you ready?" Christine asked, taking a deep breath. Both she and Lacy had brought the packages they'd received.

"I hope so." They didn't have an appointment, or any real plan. Hannah sincerely hoped they hadn't driven all this way for nothing—again. If Brian wouldn't see them, she didn't know if they would ever find answers.

Lacy lifted her chin and strolled purposefully to the door. "Here goes nothing."

Chapter Twenty-Two

The lobby at Maris & Maris was about as bland as one could be, with beige walls, beige carpet, beige chairs. The receptionist—a woman of indeterminate age who wore her dishwater-blond hair in a tidy chignon above an immaculate gray sweater—asked if they had an appointment, and when they said they didn't, she made a face.

"Mr. Maris is booked all day today," she said. "You should have made an appointment."

"I'm confident he'll want to speak to us," Christine said. "When he has a moment, please tell him Nancy Whitmore's niece is here to speak with him."

Hannah craned her neck, trying to see down a hallway that branched off behind the front desk. Was Madison there? Hannah didn't see movement.

If Nancy's name meant anything to the receptionist, she didn't give any indication. Instead, she sighed and said, "Mr. Maris is with a client right now, but if you have a seat, I will speak to him as soon as I have a chance."

"What about Madison?" Hannah asked. "Is she available?"

The receptionist pressed her lips together. "Ms. Maris does not see clients."

So she *was* here. "I bet if you tell her who we are, she'll see us," Hannah said, though she had her doubts.

"That's not how we do things here. When Mr. Maris has a break, I will speak to him." She ground out the words, somehow making them sound extremely unpleasant while maintaining a forced smile. "Have a seat if you'd like to wait. It could be a while."

They sat on the beige chairs, and Hannah scanned the small waiting area. Brian's and Craig's law degrees were hung on the wall in fancy frames. There were copies of magazines at least a year old. A dying fern dropped brown leaves on an oak side table. A clock behind the receptionist's desk ticked away the minutes.

Christine pulled out her phone and started scrolling. Lacy took a small crossword puzzle book out of her bag. Hannah had brought along a novel. Her mother had instilled in her from a very young age that she should always bring something to read. She got that out and started reading. From somewhere inside the office, she heard voices, but no one came to the front.

She tried to focus on the pages, but her thoughts kept drifting. The ticking clock echoed in the quiet room.

After what felt like an eternity, but in reality was only about forty minutes according to the clock on the wall, one of the voices grew louder, and a moment later a young man and an older woman stepped into the hallway.

"Thank you so much, Claudia, Jimmy," the receptionist said, ducking her head. "You all have a good day now."

"You too, Ruth," the woman—Claudia—said.

Hannah expected that the receptionist would let Brian know they were there, but she didn't make any move to do so. A moment later, an older man entered the reception area and she greeted him brightly. "Hello there, Willie," she said. "Mr. Maris is all ready to see you."

"Excuse me," Hannah said. "Could you please let Mr. Maris know we're here? I'm sure he'll want to take a moment to see us before his next appointment begins."

"His next appointment is already here," Ruth said, gesturing at the older man. "It would hardly be fair to make Willie wait for people who don't have an appointment, would it?"

Willie looked from her to them and back again, seemingly unsure what to do.

"It will only take a second," Lacy said. "I'm sure that if you tell Mr. Maris who we are—"

"You can go right on through, Willie," Ruth interrupted. She gestured down the hallway. "Mr. Maris is waiting for you."

"You didn't even tell him we were here," Christine said.

"As I said, Mr. Maris has a very busy schedule." Ruth had already turned to her computer again and was typing away. "If he has a free moment, I will let him know. But it wouldn't be fair to the clients who made appointments to make them wait for people who simply showed up unannounced."

Hannah took a deep breath and let it out slowly. She'd encountered plenty of people like Ruth, who had a tiny bit of power and wielded it with authority. And the woman was right. Their questions weren't so important to anyone other than themselves that they should inconvenience others.

Hannah was sure that if Brian Maris knew they were here, he would want to see them. She was also sure that—short of bursting through to the back without permission—they weren't going to see Brian until his current appointment ended.

"How long is this appointment supposed to be?" Hannah asked.

Ruth didn't look up from the screen. "Mr. Maris will be busy for an hour and a half."

What kind of appointment lasted that long? They couldn't sit there all day and simply wait. On the other hand, they had come all this way. They couldn't leave.

But then Hannah had an idea. "The old mining town—Russell. That's not far from here, is it?"

"Not far at all," Christine said. "But I don't think there's really anything left."

"It would still be cool to see it," Lacy said. "Or what's left of it."

"This says it's ten minutes away," Christine said, holding up her phone. "There are supposed to be a couple buildings still standing."

"And maybe we could also go check out your grandparents' house, the one they built after the mines closed. Where your aunt lived. That's around here too, isn't it?"

"I think so. Hang on." It took Christine a minute to locate the address and type it in, but then she said, "It's between here and the town."

"Why would we go there?" Lacy asked.

"I'd kind of like to see it," Christine said. "I haven't been there in years."

"And if we'd just be sitting here for the next hour and a half…" Hannah glanced at Ruth, who typed on her computer, as if she couldn't hear any of their conversation.

"Let's go." Christine slid her phone into her pocket as she pushed herself up.

Hannah approached the desk. "Can we make an appointment for an hour and a half from now? And is there any way you could let us know if Mr. Maris is free sooner than expected?"

"Yes, and he won't be," Ruth replied.

"Here's my phone number, just in case," Hannah said, setting her business card on the desk. "We'd very much like to talk to him. And like we said, I think he'll want to talk to us too. It has to do with a client of his."

"We'll be back before his appointment ends," Lacy added, and then they walked out.

"She wasn't very nice," Christine said as soon as they were outside.

"I'm sure she's just doing her job," Lacy said. "I mean, she can't let just anyone trot into the lawyer's office unannounced. She's right that it wouldn't be fair to the people who've made appointments."

"If this is the only law firm in town, I imagine we're not the first people to come in here hoping to talk to one of the lawyers urgently without an appointment," Hannah agreed. "She's probably been told to do exactly what she did."

"Look at you two, seeing the good in people," Christine said. "Someone raised you right, that's for sure."

Lacy laughed as they climbed into her car. "Do you have those directions ready?"

"Sure do. At least, directions to where Russell used to be."

They drove out of Harlan and onto a rural road that wound around a hill and then veered onto another side road, before descending into a valley. The road was rough, with many potholes and broken sections in the pavement. Lacy took it slow.

"It should be up that way," Christine said as they came to an intersection near a small pond. "That's Russell Road."

Hills rose around them on all sides. In the small valley, there were a couple of wooden buildings leaning precariously but somehow still standing.

"Let's go check those out." Lacy parked the car and climbed out.

Christine and Hannah followed her, and their feet crunched over the gravel of Russell Road. The first building had been painted white at one point, but was mostly weathered wood now. Its roof had largely collapsed, and the walls heaved to one side, but there was still a front door, chained and locked. Not that that was much of a deterrent for anyone who might have wanted to enter, as the windows along two walls were broken.

"'Company Store,'" Christine said, pointing to writing that had faded almost to white over the door.

"And that was a post office," Hannah said, pointing at the next building over, which was in similar shape but had US Post Office carved into a wooden sign. A flagpole stood in front, but there was no flag.

"Based on the picture I saw, the houses would have been up that way," Hannah said, pointing toward a field that sloped up from the area. "Rows and rows of small white houses."

"Shacks, more like," Christine said.

Hannah wondered which of those houses Helen and Nancy had grown up in, and where Helen and Walter had lived before they moved. There was nothing left of the houses, so that mystery would remain unsolved.

"I wonder where the mine was," Lacy said, turning around. "Perhaps the entrance is still there."

"We are not going in, even if it is," Christine said.

"No way. I'm with your mom on this one," Hannah agreed.

"Fine," Lacy said, rolling her eyes. "This place is totally depressing. Should we go see the house?"

Hannah disagreed with Lacy's assessment. She saw a kind of stark beauty here. A place where so many families had lived and laughed and persevered. A town that had seen disasters and survived strikes and struggled under the thumb of the powerful company that had kept them all in line. Coal mining had been a hard life, and many of the miners would have loved a chance to do anything else. But she also knew from Helen's diaries that there were happy memories here too.

Hannah followed Lacy to the car. This journey was about her friend, not her.

Christine had already entered the address of the house into her phone's GPS. Soon they were bumping their way out of the valley, down a side road that hugged a hill and then rose along a narrow dirt road. Hannah couldn't imagine driving this road when it snowed or there was a freeze. Luckily those events didn't happen too often in these parts.

"This looks right," Christine said. "I think it's up there on the left. We visited my grandparents when I was very young, so this is vaguely familiar."

"Didn't Nancy also live here?" Hannah asked. "She was caring for her parents. How did you manage not to meet her?"

"I don't know," Christine said. "She must have stayed away from the house or something. That's all I can think of. But I have no memory of meeting her, ever."

"What about your grandparents' funerals?" Lacy asked. "Surely you would have run into her at those?"

"I don't think she was there, at least not when we were," Christine said. "I vaguely remember hearing my parents talking about that, about how hurtful it was that she couldn't get over her anger for the funerals."

"She skipped her parents' funerals after caring for them for decades, all so she didn't have to see her sister?" Hannah couldn't imagine. How angry would someone have to be for that to be their choice?

"Maybe because she saw them every day at home, she didn't feel the need to grieve them publicly?" Christine suggested. "I don't know. I wish I'd asked more about it now, obviously, but I was a kid, so I didn't question it."

"No one lives in the house now, right?" Lacy asked.

"I don't know," Christine said.

"The property records didn't indicate a sale," Hannah said. "But I don't know other than that."

As Christine had said, a long driveway branched off to the left, and a small wooden bungalow came into view. A small yard and driveway surrounded it, with stands of beech and poplar and sweet gums all around it.

"It's cute," Lacy said. "Look at that porch."

A covered porch fronted the boxy, square house with an A-line roof. It *was* cute—or could be, with some time and attention. The yard was overgrown and filled with weeds, the gutter hung off one corner of the roof, and the porch stairs sloped at an awkward angle. There were no cars in the driveway, no toys in the yard or chairs on the porch—nothing to indicate it had been inhabited recently.

"It sure doesn't look occupied," Hannah said. Through the trees, she could make out the shape of another house, but it was far enough away that the property was sure to be quiet and relatively isolated.

"Wait until you see the view," Christine said. "I don't remember a lot about this house, but I do remember that." She climbed out of the car and walked to the house, and Lacy and Hannah followed her. She crossed the yard and made her way up the rickety porch steps. "Watch that one," she said, indicating the middle step, which sank below Hannah's foot as she followed Christine. Once they were on the porch, Hannah turned around and gasped.

They could see the whole valley from here. Beyond that, mountains rolled out, one after another, into the distance.

"This is incredible," Hannah said. The word didn't do the view justice, but she couldn't think of one that would.

"How in the world were your grandparents able to afford a view like this?" Lacy asked. "This is gorgeous."

"Don't forget how far up we are," Christine said. "Land this far off the beaten path wasn't in high demand years ago. And you saw that dirt road. It was even worse back in the day. You could get stuck up here for weeks on end if the road iced over." She gazed up at the house. "I imagine it was all they could afford."

But Hannah was thinking about something else. "Your aunt Nancy lived up here all alone until she moved into that nursing home?" Now that she saw how remote and rugged it was, it was hard to imagine a woman in her eighties living there on her own.

"As far as I know. She must have been one tough lady," Christine said. A moment later, she added, "I wish I'd known her."

Hannah approached the door and tried the handle. It was locked.

"That's too bad," Lacy said.

Hannah stepped to the side and pressed her face against a window, shading her eyes with her hands. Inside, she could see a couch, a recliner, a coffee table, and a flat-screen TV in the corner. Beyond the front room, she could see the edge of a refrigerator through an open doorway.

"I just had a crazy idea," Christine said.

"What?" Hannah asked.

"Look at that keyhole." Christine had opened her small bag and was rooting through it. Hannah had given the package back to her that morning.

Hannah leaned forward and saw what she was talking about. Instead of a typical keyhole in the door handle, this house had an old-fashioned round knob with a keyhole underneath. And the key that would fit in this keyhole was much thicker than the average key. It almost looked as if—

Christine had pulled the heavy brass key out of her bag and was inserting it into the keyhole.

Hannah held her breath as she saw it slide cleanly in. And then gasped as it began to turn.

"No way," Lacy said.

"It looks like it," Christine said, her eyes wide. And then she reached for the door handle, twisted it, and pushed the door open.

Chapter Twenty-Three

They stepped inside the house, and Hannah immediately sneezed. Everything in the place was coated in a layer of dust, but aside from that, it looked as if Aunt Nancy had gone out to the store and simply never come back. There were books and a TV remote on the coffee table. Shoes were neatly lined up by the door. A heavy wool coat hung on a hook above the shoes.

Lacy stepped into the front room and ran her finger over a bookcase beside the recliner, leaving a streak in the dust. "It's as if no one has touched it since she left."

"This place is pretty much how I remember it from when my grandparents lived here," Christine said. "The TV is new, obviously, and the furniture is different, but otherwise…" She gestured around the room before wandering down the hallway, and Hannah and Lacy followed her into the kitchen. There was a fridge, a sink, butcher-block countertops, and cabinets painted a cheerful blue. A scarred wooden table stood in the middle of the room, but there were only two chairs around it.

"The bedrooms are over here," Christine said. She headed down the hallway to the back of the house.

"Okay," Lacy said from behind her. "Why would your aunt send you a key to unlock a house you haven't been to in decades?"

"The house she lived in, until she couldn't," Hannah added.

"And what do the handkerchiefs and poem have to do with anything?" Lacy added.

"I wish I knew," Christine murmured.

Hannah had an idea. While Lacy and Christine continued to the rear of the house, she went back to the front room. Next to the recliner, which was positioned in the corner facing the TV, stood a bookshelf. The one that now had Lacy's fingerprint streaked in the dust on top. Hannah crouched in front of it and scanned the spines. Several Bibles, a few Bible study books, a couple of mysteries, and…there it was.

Sure enough, she spotted a volume of Emily Dickinson's poetry on the top shelf. Hannah slid it out, set it on top of the bookshelf, and let it fall open—right to poem 1383. The now-familiar words leaped from the page.

Long Years apart — can make no
Breach a second cannot fill —

This poem had meant something to Nancy, there was no doubt about it. And Hannah was pretty certain that it had something to do with the estrangement between Nancy and her sister. But what message was Nancy trying to give to Lacy and Christine? Why would she send this poem, and this key, and—

"Hannah?" Lacy called from somewhere at the other end of the house. "You should come see this."

"Coming," Hannah replied. She hurried toward the sound of her friend's voice. What had they found?

She was relieved to see that there was nothing visibly wrong in the rear bedroom, where Lacy stood with her mother. There was a full-size bed with a lacy cover, a nightstand with a lamp and another Bible, a dresser crowded with black-and-white photos on top, and a small table with a—

Now she saw what they were looking at. On the table was a small chest, about the size of a bread box. It had a rounded top and a lock on the front. Above the lock was a round metal insert with the shape of a mountain pressed into it. It matched the symbol on the keys.

"Try your key again," Lacy said to Christine.

Christine fitted her key into the hole then shook her head. "It won't turn. Good thing we have another key."

Lacy took out her key and inserted it into the hole. She twisted it, and there was a satisfying *click* as the chest unlocked. Lacy opened the top.

"Oh my," Christine said, lifting a handful of photographs from the chest. "What is all this?"

Lacy gasped as she drew out a newspaper clipping. "This is an article from the *Blackberry Valley Chronicle* about my egg business." It showed a picture of Lacy in front of her henhouse, and the story mentioned how she was transforming the old cattle farm into an egg business. It had run the previous summer.

"These are photos of you and me." Christine set the pictures down and spread them out on the bed. There was a photo of Christine as a toddler, above another that might have been her senior photo, with her hair long and straight around her shoulders. One of the pictures was Lacy's senior photo, with fringed bangs and layered hair, and another was her engagement photo from the newspaper.

"They're all photocopies, or cut from newspapers," Lacy observed, and Hannah realized she was right.

"Where did all this come from?" Christine asked, reaching into the box to retrieve a clipping of an interview Christine had given to the *Blackberry Valley Chronicle* after her zucchini had won a blue ribbon at the county fair in 1997.

"Is it all stuff about you and me?" Lacy asked.

"Not all of it." Christine held out a newspaper clipping. "This is from the *Lexington Herald Leader* in 2009. Mom is interviewed in this article, talking about her feelings on a proposed neighborhood rezoning." She gave a small smile. "She sounds as practical and sharp as she ever did." The smile faded from her face. "And here is her obituary."

"Nancy collected all this stuff about us," Lacy said, her fingers trembling as she held the clippings. "I thought she didn't even know I existed, but she's been following me my whole life." She looked at her senior photo again. "Why would she collect all this stuff and not just, you know, reach out to say hello? If I'd known she cared, I would have made sure to send her things myself to keep her in the loop. I would have built a relationship with her."

"Maybe she was afraid?" Hannah suggested. "Of being rejected?"

"Why would I reject my great-aunt?" Lacy asked. "Her problem was with Grandma, not with me. She and I were family."

"But we never reached out either," Christine said. "Maybe that was why she was afraid. My whole life, I knew Mom had a sister, but I never bothered to try to find her. I don't know why I didn't. My mom didn't get along with her, but that didn't mean I couldn't have met her. I suppose I was afraid of opening old wounds. I didn't want to disrupt her life if there was a chance she didn't want me in it."

"Families are complicated." Hannah was trying not to insert herself into what Lacy and Christine were going through at that moment, but she couldn't help offering the sentiment, trying to ease their hurt.

"She kept all this stuff from Grandma too," Lacy said, pulling more envelopes and photographs out of the box. "Here are some letters Grandma sent to her parents from Lexington." She opened one and a yellowed snapshot of Christine as a toddler fell out. "Even after her parents passed away, she kept all of this about the sister she no longer spoke to."

"By all appearances, Nancy never stopped loving my mom, and by extension, us," Christine said softly. "Why else would she collect and keep all this stuff?"

"But if she cared so much, why not reach out to us?" Lacy asked. "Even if she couldn't bring herself to make amends with Grandma, why didn't she find us after Grandma was gone instead of just keeping a box of clippings?"

"My question is why did she arrange to have you all find this here after she passed?" Hannah said. "I can buy that for whatever reason—fear, insecurity, or even inertia—she didn't want to make contact. But then why leave it all here for you to find once she passed? Because that's what she did, right? She must have directed that those envelopes be delivered to you both in her will. That's why Maris & Maris had Madison deliver them, right?"

"I believe so," Christine said.

"So why did she do that?" Hannah pressed.

"And why not make it clear who sent it?" Lacy added.

"Or what we were supposed to do with them?" Christine asked. "But I will say this. Without your help, Hannah, there's a good chance we never would have figured out what the poem was, what the keys unlocked, or even that we'd read those handkerchiefs upside down."

"And if we hadn't found those diaries in the attic, we wouldn't have known about the handkerchiefs, or about what had happened to separate the sisters in the first place," Hannah said. "You made sure those weren't thrown away so that we could do that."

"Let's not praise my pack-rat tendencies," Christine said with a chuckle.

"If she was sending us a message, Nancy could have made it clear," Lacy said.

"So why didn't she?" Hannah said. "She must have had a reason."

"And what *was* the message?" Christine reached into the chest again and tugged out something in a sealed manila envelope. Even from where she was standing, Hannah could see a very official-looking seal on the lip.

Hannah was on the verge of asking about it when the sound of sirens screeched toward the house.

"What in the world?" Christine led the way down the hallway to the front door.

Hannah could see through the front window that two police cars had parked in the driveway and officers were approaching the house.

"Police," one of them called as he neared the home. "We need you to come outside."

Hannah didn't hesitate. She followed Lacy and Christine outside. It was surreal seeing two police officers in front of them, intent on making sure they didn't get away. Hannah's mind raced. Was this all for *them*? Were they somehow wrong about who the house belonged to? She supposed they didn't technically have permission to be there, but surely since it was Christine's aunt's house—

"Is anyone else inside?" The officer in front had dark hair and a mustache, and he peered behind the women to see who else might come out.

"It's just us," Christine said. "There's no one else here."

"I need you to come off the porch," the officer said.

"Can I ask what the problem is?" Christine said as they complied. "This is my aunt's house."

"A neighbor called to say someone was breaking and entering at the old Whitmore place," the other officer informed them.

"Technically we are guilty of entering," Christine said. "But there was no breaking involved."

"We have a key," Lacy added as she reached the bottom step.

"You have a key?" This news appeared to throw the officer. "How?"

"Like I said, it's my aunt's house," Christine said. "My aunt's name was Nancy Whitmore. I can show you the key if you like. It's inside the house."

The officer glanced at her colleague, and then at the three women. "Why don't you show me?" she asked Christine. "The rest of you stay out here."

Christine started for the door. But as they were about to head inside, they heard the sound of another car racing up the dirt road.

They all paused, and a moment later a silver BMW roared up the driveway.

"Who's that?" the officer asked.

"I have no idea," Christine said.

But Hannah could guess. She'd seen that car parked in front of a house with a mansard roof. Her suspicions were confirmed when Madison stepped out of the passenger side of the vehicle and a man Hannah recognized from his website as Brian Maris climbed out of the driver's side. One officer turned to the new arrivals, while another kept Hannah, Lacy, and Christine in his sights.

"What seems to be the trouble here?" Brian said.

"What are you doing here, Brian?" the male officer asked.

Hannah had been wondering that herself. He was supposed to be in the middle of a meeting at his office. Perhaps the meeting had run short, or Ruth had relented and passed on the message about who they were and where they were headed. They'd been right—he very much wanted to see them.

Brian greeted both officers. "Hi, Phillip. Good to see you. Heather, you're looking well."

Madison was wide-eyed, staring from Hannah and Lacy and Christine to the officers.

"This house was owned by one of my clients, a Miss Nancy Whitmore," Brian said.

"This woman tells me the house is owned by her aunt," Phillip said. "Says she has a key."

"As it turns out, she's partly correct," Brian said. "She does indeed have a key. But the house doesn't belong to her aunt."

"What do you mean?" Phillip eyed him warily.

"Yes, what do you mean?" Christine echoed.

"You're Christine Johnston, right?" Brian said. "And you're Lacy Minyard?"

They both nodded.

"I thought so. As it happens, the house belongs to the two of you."

Chapter Twenty-Four

There was a lot of confusion after Brian's announcement, along with several questions, and it took a moment for him to calm everyone so that he could explain. He convinced the police there had been no break-in, so they left. Finally, he invited Christine, Lacy, and Hannah into the house so he could give them the full story.

Once everyone was seated in the living room, Christine said, "I'm glad you were able to fit us into your schedule today, Mr. Maris. Your receptionist told us that you were booked all day."

Brian winced. "Sorry for the confusion there. She was referring to my brother, Craig. She tends to call us both Mr. Maris, so sometimes we have mix-ups about which of us a client is there to see."

The lawyer began his tale. "Nancy Whitmore was my client. She lived in this house from the time her parents built it in 1965 until she went into a nursing home last spring. She took ownership of the home when her parents passed. Her sister, Helen, received a smaller inheritance, as stipulated in the will." He watched them, as if waiting for someone to object.

"That's only fair," Christine said. "After all, Nancy cared for her parents for decades."

"That's true. My father handled that inheritance, but when he retired, I took on Nancy as my client. Nancy was greatly pained by the distance that had grown between her and her sister and tried to reach out to reconcile a few times over the years. Her efforts, as I understand it, were rebuffed."

"Mom refused to reconcile with her sister?" Christine said. "That's not the way I heard it."

"That is what was reported to me by my client," Brian said.

"I never found any record of Nancy reaching out when I went through Mom's things after she passed," Christine said. Hannah suspected she was trying to understand why Brian's version of events didn't match up to what she had always believed. "I was under the impression it was Nancy who didn't want to reconcile."

Brian shrugged. "Since they've both passed, I don't know if we'll ever get the whole story. Maybe you'll find something in this house that will help you make sense of it."

"There's a whole stack of journals in her closet," Madison said. "I didn't look through them, so I don't know what's in them, but maybe you'll find something in there."

"This is my daughter, Madison," Brian said. "She's working for me this summer."

Hannah smiled at the young woman. "We've met."

"Sorry I ran away the other day," she said sheepishly. "I was given strict instructions not to talk to either of you, so when you showed up at the lake, I panicked."

"In addition to running errands for me, Madison also collected the items Nancy directed us to send to you," Brian said. "She had to poke around the house a bit to find them all. I don't know what's in her journals, but I know Nancy never stopped caring for her sister, and she followed the lives of her niece and great-niece as best she could throughout her life."

"I wasn't aware that she knew I existed," Lacy said.

"She very much did. She instructed our firm to subscribe to the *Blackberry Valley Chronicle* and send along any clipping that mentioned either one of you," Brian said. "Which we did."

"But she never reached out to make contact with us," Christine said.

"I was under the impression she'd been given strict instructions by her sister to leave you all alone," Brian said. "Again, there's no way to know the truth, but that's what I was told. In any case, she followed your lives. And once her sister died, she changed her will to leave the house to you."

"She never had any other family?" Hannah asked. It saddened her to think about Nancy up here on this hill all alone, pining away for family she couldn't be in touch with. Having no one to leave her home to but a niece she hadn't seen in so many years.

"Nancy never made a family of her own," Brian said. "I don't know whether she wanted to. I never asked. It's my job to make sure my clients' wishes are carried out, not to pry into the decisions behind them."

Madison spoke again. "I think there's a tactful way to do both. You can follow the spirit of the wish better if you understand it completely. You should have asked your receptionist. She probably knew Nancy's full story before she even sat down. I know I would have."

"I believe you," Brian said with a chuckle. "And like I always said, you're welcome to join the firm at any point after you get that law degree."

Madison wrinkled her nose. "No thanks."

"Well, until that day, our clients are stuck with my brother and me, and I'm afraid he's even less prone to chitchat than I am." Brian turned to Christine and Lacy. "What I do know is that Nancy came to my office about a year ago. Her health had been worsening, and the doctors wanted to move her into a home that would allow for regular care. She wouldn't hear of it. Nancy had a nurse who came to check on her every day and insisted that was good enough for her. She said the good Lord would call her home when He was ready, and there wasn't anything to be done about it."

"I admire that," Christine said.

"She was quite the character," Brian said with a smile. "She did have to move to a home eventually, after she had a stroke and couldn't remain on her own. But she was fiercely independent for as long as she could be."

"I wish I'd been able to know her." Christine ducked her head, but not before Hannah saw her chin tremble. Lacy took her mom's hand, and Christine gave her a grateful smile.

No one said anything for a moment. Hannah thought about how pride and hurt feelings had kept this family torn apart for so long. She resolved never to let anything come between herself and the people she loved.

"When she called me last year, she knew her time was getting close," Brian said. "She told me she wanted her niece and great-niece to know her when she was gone, but more than that, she wanted to find a way to make sure you weren't driven apart the way she and her sister were. She was planning to leave you the house, but she also wanted to make sure you both had to be here to claim it."

Hannah straightened in her seat. "That's why one key opened the door and the other opened the chest."

"Apparently that chest was a gift from the Russell Mining Company to mark her father's thirtieth year in the mines," Brian said. "I have no idea why they gave him something like that. Most people get a clock or a watch for a significant anniversary."

"You would think a raise or health insurance might have been better received," Lacy said, almost under her breath.

"Yes, well, I suppose that wasn't on offer," Brian said. "But she had the chest, and she had the idea that it would be nice to have you two come here together to find the documents that left the house to you."

Christine sighed. "I suppose I can see how she thought that might be a good idea. But here's what I don't understand, and it's a question we've probably asked a hundred times since these envelopes showed up. Why did she send such random stuff? I mean, the keys make sense now, but that took a while. And what about everything else? The handkerchiefs? The poem? Why was everything so cryptic? Why not simply send us a note telling us where to find the chest?"

"That might have been my fault," Madison said, grimacing. "I'm sorry. I didn't mean to mess things up. My dad sent me up here to retrieve the things Nancy wanted to send to you all—"

"So Aunt Nancy didn't put the packages together before she passed?" Christine asked.

"No," Brian said. "But she left instructions for what she wanted to include. It took several months for everything to clear probate, but once it did, I sent Madison up here to gather the items."

"It wasn't hard to find the things she wanted to include," Madison said. "They were all in the top drawer of her dresser like she said they'd be. She'd written out her favorite Emily Dickinson poem, and I found that, along with the keys and the handkerchiefs." She flinched. "What I missed, though, were the notes that were supposed to be included in the packages as well."

"So there *was* supposed to be an explanation?" Lacy's eyes were wide.

"Definitely." Madison hung her head. "I didn't realize I'd missed those until you showed up in Harlan on Sunday. I couldn't figure out why you came to see me instead of stopping by the office as the note instructed. But then I thought it through, and I realized the notes hadn't been in the packages I dropped off after all. I was so excited about the trip to Blackberry Valley that I completely spaced on the notes."

Brian's expression indicated this was news to him. "You ladies didn't know who the packages were from?"

"We figured it out eventually, but it took a lot of work," Christine said.

"And my brilliant best friend, Hannah, who did most of the sleuthing," Lacy added.

"I am so sorry," he said. He faced his daughter. "So where are the notes?"

"Probably still in the dresser drawer," Madison said. "Should I go check?"

"Yes, please." The exasperation Brian felt was barely masked by his calm tone. Madison hopped up and hurried out of the room. "There was supposed to be a business card for my office as well,"

Brian said to the women, raking his hands through his hair. "I'm guessing that didn't make it into the envelopes either."

"Nope," Lacy said.

He made a noise at the back of his throat. "My daughter is so smart, but she can also be a bit flighty." He grimaced. "I am so sorry for all the trouble. I was beginning to wonder why I hadn't heard from you, but it's become quite clear."

"She's young," Christine said gently. "We're all flighty when we're young."

"Besides, I get the sense that law isn't her dream career," Hannah added.

"Not really," Brian said.

"Give her time," Christine said. "One day you'll realize your daughter is a grown woman with her own life, and you'll long for the days she couldn't be trusted to stuff an envelope." She smiled at Lacy, who beamed.

"If you say so." Brian looked dubious. "I still feel terrible for the confusion. She told me delivering them went fine. Is that true, at least?"

"If all she was supposed to do was get them to the right places, then, yes, she did that," Hannah said with a laugh. "No one was served or anything like that, if that's what you mean."

"No, thankfully not," Brian said, shaking his head. "Nancy wanted them hand-delivered, not sent in the mail. She didn't trust that they would make it through the postal service unscathed."

"They didn't make it unscathed this way either," Christine said with a chuckle. "We had some trouble reading the poem because the ink had run."

Brian repeated the noise he'd made a moment before. "She did tell me that her enormous travel cup spilled and one of the packages had gotten a little wet. She didn't tell me the package had *opened* and gotten wet."

"She's young," Christine repeated as Madison returned with two small envelopes.

"Here you go," she said sheepishly, handing one each to Christine and Lacy.

"Maybe you can answer another question for me," Christine said. "Why did my envelope say it was from Lacy, while hers said it was from me?"

"That was my own touch," Madison said. "I thought it would get your attention, getting packages from each other that neither had actually sent."

"It certainly did that," Christine said.

Lacy slid her finger under the flap of the envelope that Madison had handed her. Her name was scrawled on it in the same spidery handwriting that the poem had been written in.

Hannah scooted closer to read over Lacy's shoulder.

> *Dear Lacy,*
>
> *We've never met, but I've followed your life since you were born, and it is the greatest sadness of my life that we were not able to become acquainted. I'm your grandmother's sister, and she and I had a falling-out many years ago. I pray that you will never lose touch with someone you love as dearly as I loved my sister.*

The enclosed handkerchief is one that she helped me make many years ago. It serves as a reminder of happier times for me. I am also sending you this key, as I have sent one to your mother, in hopes that it will bring you two together. You'll find the chest that it unlocks in my home. I hope you'll be pleased with what you find inside.

With love,

Your Great-Aunt Nancy

After Lacy read her note, she exchanged hers with the one addressed to Christine. It had essentially the same wording, except in this one she revealed that she had included her favorite Emily Dickinson poem because it spoke to a love that never dies between friends—or sisters—even separated by hurt feelings. She added that she prayed Christine and Lacy would never find themselves separated like she and her sister had been.

"So she wanted us to come up here to find the clippings and pictures she'd kept all this time?" Lacy asked after they'd read the notes.

"Yes, but they weren't the only things in that box," Brian said.

"Funnily enough, we didn't get a chance to go through everything in the box because the police arrived," Christine said wryly.

"Why don't you go see what else is in that box now?" Brian suggested.

Christine left the room and returned a moment later, holding a manila envelope with an official-looking seal.

"Go ahead and open that, although I'm afraid I've already ruined the surprise," Brian said.

"It's the deed to the house, isn't it?" Christine broke the seal with her index finger.

"It is. This all belongs to you two now," Brian said, gesturing around the small room. "Which, again, was part of your aunt's plan. Because you *both* own it, you'll need to decide together what to do with it."

"Oh my," Christine said.

"It would make a great vacation place," Madison said. "With a view like that? I bet you could list it on a website for people to rent for getaways."

"There's plenty of good hunting nearby," Brian added. "Or one or both of you could choose to live here. It's not a bad place."

Hannah knew that Lacy would never leave the farm, and she suspected the idea wouldn't appeal to Christine either. But it wasn't her place to say so.

Christine took Lacy's hand, and the two exchanged glances. Hannah had a pretty good idea she knew what they had already decided. If they sold the house, there would be money to fix up the cottage on the farm, which was what they both wanted.

Brian checked his watch. "Unfortunately, I need to get going. I have another client waiting at the office. We'll set up an appointment to work through all the details. There are lots of forms to fill out, as you might expect. But please give me a call if you have any questions in the meantime. Or if you decide what you want to do with the house."

"We will," Christine assured him.

"Thank you for everything," Lacy added.

"Of course. I'm sorry again that it was more confusing than it needed to be," Brian said.

"Very sorry," Madison chimed in. Then father and daughter said their goodbyes and slipped out of the house.

Once it was just the three of them in the small house, Lacy and Christine and Hannah sat in the living room for a moment, taking it all in.

"She really left us this house," Lacy said.

"It seems she did," Christine agreed. "But even more importantly, she cared about us. My whole life, I never really thought much about her. And it looks as though she spent my whole life keeping tabs on me, and then you."

"I wish we'd known that," Lacy said. "I wish we'd known her."

"It's such a shame, isn't it?" Christine took in a deep breath and let it out slowly. "If it's true that my mom asked her never to be in contact with us, that's a tragedy. I hope I never let a disagreement or misunderstanding get in the way of a relationship with someone I love."

"Me too," Lacy said. "All I want is for the people I love to be closer."

Christine beamed at her. "I want that too."

Hannah couldn't agree more. Even though she didn't always see eye to eye with everyone in her family—even though she sometimes wanted to scream when her friends and family tried to interfere with her love life—she knew, deep down, that it came from a good place. That it meant they loved her and wanted her to be happy. She'd been gone for so long and missed so much time with her loved ones.

"Isn't it funny how nothing about those envelopes made sense a week ago, but now that we know what happened and what they were supposed to do, it all comes together?" Christine asked.

"There's always an answer to every puzzle," Lacy said.

"It's just that sometimes you have to look at things a little differently to see it," Hannah added.

After a few minutes, Christine pushed herself up and walked out onto the porch. Lacy and Hannah followed a few steps behind.

"It really is stunning, isn't it?" Lacy said, looking out over the valley below.

"It's breathtaking," Hannah agreed. From here she could see nothing but mountains cloaked in green foliage, rolling out endlessly into the distance. It felt like she could see forever. As if way up here, she was a little closer to God.

"It will be hard to let this go," Christine said.

"But it will be worth it to have you close by," Lacy said.

"If that's what you want," Christine said.

Lacy faced her mother and took both of her hands. "Mom, that's what I've always wanted. It isn't right for you to live in a tiny apartment in town. The farm doesn't feel the same without you."

"But you deserve to make it your own. I can't get in the way of that."

"You won't," Lacy insisted. "With you in the cottage and us in the main house, we'll each have our own space, but we'll still be as close as I want us to be. You'll be near enough to remember Dad in the house and on the property whenever you want, but you'll have a fresh start in the cottage."

Christine's eyes sparkled with unshed tears. "But—"

"No." Lacy cut her off firmly. "No more buts. Come *home*, Mom."

Christine peered into her daughter's eyes for another moment then threw her arms around Lacy and held her close. "Thank you, Lacy. I will."

"You better," Lacy replied, her voice muffled in Christine's shoulder.

And just like that, it was settled. Helen and Nancy might have missed most of each other's lives, but Christine and Lacy were not going to let that happen to them. Hannah suspected it was exactly what Nancy had been hoping for, even though there was no way she could have known her niece and great-niece's situation.

The three women stood there for a long time, admiring the view. Hannah knew they should get going soon. That they had a long drive ahead of them. That there was so much to do and think about.

But for now, she was content to take in the mountains God had made and appreciate the beauty that was all around them. She hoped she would never take it for granted. She hoped she would never forget to hold the people she loved close.

She hoped she would never forget to thank God for bringing her home to be a part of all of this.

From the Author

Dear Reader,

Writing a story set in a fictional town like Blackberry Valley is an author's delight. We can arrange the buildings to suit ourselves, put the stoplights anywhere we want, and create as many fun shops and restaurants as our imaginations can provide. The fun gets even better when we work with other authors whose books are set in the same fanciful town, as is the case with the Mysteries of Blackberry Valley. When you put a bunch of inventive writers together and tell them, "Create a series!" the ideas flow and blend in amazing ways. The result is better than any of us could devise on our own. I was so excited to be invited to be a part of this venture.

Since I was born and raised in central Kentucky, I was eager to ensure that my home state was portrayed with all the rich beauty, charm, and quirkiness that are prevalent in actual small towns in the Bluegrass State. Let me assure you, Blackberry Valley represents rural Kentucky well, which is one of the reasons I love this series so much. When you read these books, you'll feel like you've visited the beautiful state I call home.

And don't even get me started on the food! Hot Browns are a long-standing Kentucky tradition, and chefs across the state are fiercely proud of their unique twists on the recipe. The legendary open-faced sandwich originated at the Brown Hotel in Louisville, Kentucky, in the 1920's. The hotel was a local hotspot, sometimes serving as many as 1,200 hungry people in the early morning hours after a night of dancing and merrymaking. The typical post-party meal was ham and eggs, but people grew tired of it. As an alternative, Chef Fred K. Schmidt created the first Hot Brown, which was an instant hit. It's one of my all-time favorite dishes.

In this book I had the great pleasure of partnering with Beth Adams. King Solomon said in Ecclesiastes, "Two are better than one..." and this book proves that piece of wisdom to be true. Thank you, Beth.

I hope you enjoy your visit to Kentucky!

Virginia Smith

About the Authors

Virginia Smith

Bestselling author Virginia Smith's first novel was published in 2006. Since then, she's written more than fifty books that have collected a satisfying number of accolades and awards including two Holt Medallion Awards of Merit and a *Library Journal* top pick. A Kentucky native, Ginny loves to introduce readers to the Bluegrass State in her books (where the grass is green, not blue!). She and her husband live in central Kentucky with a feisty Maltese watchdog named Max.

Beth Adams

Beth Adams lives in Brooklyn, New York, with her husband and two daughters. When she's not writing, she's trying to find time to read mysteries.

The Hot Spotlight

The humble handkerchief has fallen out of style these days, but it has a fascinating history. Historians have found evidence that cultures all around the world have used handkerchiefs for thousands of years. Archaeologists have found images of figures holding small cloths from 1000 BC in China, and Romans were known to wave handkerchiefs in the air as a way to start chariot races.

Handkerchiefs were also used in Middle Eastern cultures and around the world, though not always for blowing noses. They were used for signaling others, for wiping brows, for holding coins, and for decorative purposes. During the Middle Ages, wealthy individuals and kings often carried elaborately embroidered handkerchiefs as a status symbol.

Handkerchiefs have also been used as a symbol of love or devotion. Knights were said to tie certain ladies' handkerchiefs to their helmets as a token of good luck. In the Renaissance, if a woman presented a man with her handkerchief, that was her way of saying she was interested in him. By accepting, men were saying the interest was mutual. If something happened to their romantic interest, he would send the handkerchief back—the classical equivalent of a modern breakup. Ladies were said to drop their handkerchiefs on the ground to signal that they were looking for love, and tossing them out of windows to gain the attention of their love interest. In

Shakespeare's *Othello*, the titular character gives a handkerchief to Desdemona as a symbol of fidelity, and when he thinks she has given it to someone else, the tragic plot is set in motion.

Handkerchiefs continued to be quite the fashion accessory and status symbol, often made from exotic materials and lavishly decorated. They also grew in size in eighteenth-century France, at least until King Louis XVI declared that no one was allowed to have a handkerchief larger than his own and decreed how large handkerchiefs could be. When it became fashionable for men to wear two-piece suits in the nineteenth century, a pocket to display a handkerchief became standard.

As mass production took over in the twentieth century, handkerchiefs were made of cheaper materials and produced more quickly. And when the flu pandemic of 1918 hit, disposable tissues grew in popularity as a way to stop the spread of germs. Handkerchiefs fell out of fashion, and while they have not disappeared, they are more commonly used as a fashion accessory than for practical purposes these days. Though I think we can all agree that using this classic symbol of love to draw a family closer together, as happened in our story, is one of the most practical purposes imaginable.

From the Hot Spot Kitchen

HANNAH'S KENTUCKY HOT BROWNS

(serves 4)

Ingredients:

For the blackberry compote:

2 cups fresh blackberries

¼ cup white sugar

1 teaspoon lemon juice

Pinch of salt

For the sandwiches:

4 tablespoons butter, divided

2 tablespoons flour

2 cups whole milk

1¾ cup shredded white cheddar cheese (divided)

¾ cup grated parmesan (divided)

Pinch of nutmeg

A few dashes hot sauce

2 sliced ripe tomatoes

A few dashes olive oil

4 slices bread (ideally a good bread, sliced thick, though any bread will do)

1 pound sliced roasted turkey

8 slices thick-cut bacon, cooked until crisp

Pinch of paprika

Chopped parsley for garnish

Salt and pepper to taste

Directions:

Start with blackberry compote. Place all ingredients in saucepan. Bring to a boil, then reduce heat to medium and simmer until sauce has reduced and thickened, about 15 to 20 minutes. Remove from heat and cool.

For Mornay sauce, melt 2 tablespoons butter in large pan and stir in flour. Cook for one minute, and then add milk a little at a time, stirring until incorporated after each addition. Cook until sauce simmers and is thickened, 3 to 5 minutes. Remove from heat and whisk in 1 cup shredded cheddar cheese and ½ cup parmesan until melted. Season with nutmeg, hot sauce, salt, and pepper.

Turn oven to broil. Arrange tomato slices on sheet pan and sprinkle with salt, pepper, and olive oil. Roast until lightly charred, about a minute on each side.

Butter bread slices with remaining butter and arrange on foil-lined baking sheet. Toast under broiler for a couple of minutes on each side. Top toasted bread with turkey, bacon, tomato, and sauce, and sprinkle with remaining cheese. Broil 2 to 3 minutes. Transfer to plates and top with blackberry compote. Sprinkle with parsley and a bit of paprika.

Read on for a sneak peek of another exciting book
in the *Mysteries of Blackberry Valley* series!

Seeds of Suspicion

BY ELIZABETH PENNEY

G rowing up, one of Hannah Prentiss's favorite activities had been
taking a leisurely bike ride through the countryside around her
hometown of Blackberry Valley, Kentucky. Nothing was better than
the sun on her face, the wind in her hair, and views of fields and
woods unspooling as she pedaled along a winding rural road.

On this fine August Monday, as the owner of a farm-to-table
restaurant called the Hot Spot, Hannah's drive had a purpose. She
was on her way to the King Farm, owned by Elaine Wilby, who also
worked as the hostess at Hannah's restaurant. Elaine grew berries
and vegetables, and as part of Hannah's commitment to local farms,
she was personally picking up a small order. While the produce,
meat, and dairy were usually delivered, she enjoyed visiting her sup-
pliers now and then, walking through the fields or barns, patting
cows and tasting samples.

Especially tasting samples.

As she signaled and turned into a long driveway marked by an
open gate and a faded painted sign, her mouth watered. Blackberries

were in, and they were her primary interest today. She needed them for the Blackberry Festival Chef Cook-Off that was happening at the end of the week.

As she approached the simple, two-story gray farmhouse with its navy blue shutters, the front door opened and Elaine stepped out onto the porch. Grinning widely, she waved and then waited while Hannah parked on the edge of the main drive.

Elaine wore a faded red bandanna over brown hair threaded with gray, jeans, a sleeveless blouse, and red garden clogs. Quite a difference from the sleek, sophisticated Elaine who served as the Hot Spot hostess every evening. About ten years older than Hannah's thirty-five, Elaine was a widow with a college-age son named Blake. He was headed to the University of Kentucky for his freshman year in a couple of weeks.

"Can I get you some sweet tea?" Elaine called as Hannah got out of the car.

"After," Hannah said. "Business before pleasure." She knew that Elaine would also have something delectable and home-baked to offer.

Elaine hopped off the porch to join Hannah. "That's fine. I already picked and packed what you ordered. Want to drive to the barn?"

"Sure."

Hannah heard scratching and whining behind the front door below the half-screen. "Hold on." With a shake of her head, Elaine returned to the house and opened the door again. Banjo, a medium-size mutt with floppy ears and a black spot around one eye, bounded out, his tail going a mile a minute. Elaine had recently adopted

Banjo from a local animal shelter. So far, it was a match made in heaven.

Elaine and Banjo climbed into the front seat, and they set off for the red main barn.

"How is everything?" Hannah asked.

To her surprise, the normally cheerful Elaine scowled. "You know that article Marshall wrote about my farm?"

Marshall Fredericks was a food critic for the local newspaper. His article entitled BLACKBERRY VALLEY'S FAMOUS LOST ONION— AND QUEEN had been a departure for him as more of a historical feature. To Marshall's delight, papers across the country had picked it up.

"I loved it," Hannah said. "Who knew onions used to be so big around here? Not to mention the Onion Queens. What a hoot." Years ago, Blackberry Valley held an annual Onion Festival to celebrate a once important crop. The last festival had been in 1932.

Elaine leaned her elbow on the window ledge and propped her chin on her fist. "That part was fine. I wish I hadn't mentioned that the Blackberry Red seeds were around here somewhere. I've had tons of calls ever since the article went national. People want to buy them from me, including some hotshot professor from Virginia. He wants to add the onion to his vegetable heritage project."

Hannah pulled up in front of the barn. Banjo immediately started barking, launching himself at the open window on Elaine's side. "Easy there," she said, grabbing his collar with one hand and unlatching the door with the other.

Once they were out, she let go of his collar, and he bolted through the open barn door.

Elaine called him, but when he didn't return, she rolled her eyes and sighed. "I'd better go grab him. There's a bunch of stuff in there he could get into."

Hannah followed her into the barn. Elaine didn't keep any farm animals, so the space was dedicated to her produce business. In one corner, she'd set up a washing station and packing area. Several glass-front refrigerators, a couple of chest freezers, and tables stored produce for distribution. Shelves held preserves, pickles, and jams Elaine made for sale from excess fruit and vegetables.

Banjo was in another area of the barn, where old horse and cow stalls still stood. He nosed at something on the worn wooden boards.

"Give me that," Elaine said, bending to pick up the item. It was a blue baseball cap with a University of Kentucky emblem. She dusted it off against her leg. "I wonder where this came from." She snorted. "Probably Blake. I tell him he sheds like a molting chicken."

Hannah laughed. Her own mother had said something similar when she and her brother were teenagers.

Elaine hung the cap on a nail. "Let's go out to the garden." She picked up two berry baskets. "We'll try some blackberries right out of the patch."

They walked out of the barn in the direction of the fields. The growing area included an extensive stand of blackberry bushes to the far left, rows of crops, and a hoop house Elaine used to start vegetables. A small cabin, the original home on the farm, stood under an ancient red maple. A young man with curly blond hair sat on the cabin steps, strumming a guitar.

"Excuse me," Elaine said. "I need to go talk to Phoenix."

Hannah stayed where she was, enjoying the day and the views across the rolling fields. From where she stood she could see the next farm, which featured a stately three-story house with a sweeping veranda. She recalled that the Combs family lived there.

Although she couldn't make out individual words, Hannah could tell that Elaine was displeased with the young man. Hands on hips, she leaned over him as she talked.

After laying aside his guitar, Phoenix put his hands up. Him, she could hear clearly. "I'm just waiting for Blake. He ran to town to pick something up. I promise we'll get it all done."

Elaine made a reply, chin bobbing in emphasis, and started back toward Hannah. Behind her, Phoenix ducked into the cabin, guitar in hand.

"Sorry," Elaine said when she reached Hannah. "He's a good kid, but I have to stay on him every minute."

Hannah clucked in sympathy. Having worked in restaurants with a wide variety of employees, she understood the frustration. "Where did he come from?"

"I put an ad on a farming group page, and he was the only one to respond. All the other potential farmhands had already been snapped up. That was my mistake. Next year, I'll advertise earlier."

"It's nice that you've given him a place to stay." Hannah glanced over her shoulder at the cabin. Phoenix marched to the barn, head ducked, wearing a ball cap and sunglasses against the hot sun.

"Wow," Hannah said when they arrived at the blackberry patch. Elaine grew a popular variety called Triple Crown. The thornless canes required trellises to support the large, juicy berries.

Thornless berries ripened later than thorny varieties, so they were the focus of the Blackberry Festival.

Elaine grinned. "Aren't they gorgeous? Go ahead, try one."

Hannah popped a blackberry into her mouth. A sweet, sun-ripened, slightly tart flavor washed over her taste buds. "Yum." Visions of how she could use this stellar fruit in recipes flooded her mind. Blackberries had always been a favorite of hers ever since she'd invented one of her most popular dishes: blackberry burrata pizza with fresh basil.

A lanky figure came running across the field in their direction. Elaine's son, Blake. Hannah always thought the handsome young man resembled his mother with his dark hair and deep brown eyes. Banjo greeted him with leaps of joy.

"Good boy, Banjo," Blake said, rubbing the dog's ears. He looked up. "Hey, Hannah."

"How are you?" Hannah asked. "Enjoying the summer?"

Blake's eyes lit with eagerness. "For the most part, yeah. I've been horseback riding a lot with my girlfriend, Kylie Jacobs. And we go swimming, kayaking, four-wheeling, and bike riding with our friends. So, yeah, I'm busy."

"Plus working," Elaine put in, her voice teasing.

"In between our fun," Blake teased back. "I wanted to check in with you and see what the priorities should be."

Elaine had a ready answer. "Please review the board for orders that have to go out today and load the truck. You two can make deliveries after lunch. Except Hannah's order. She's taking that with her."

"You got it." Blake nudged Hannah. "By the way, Kylie is running for Blackberry Queen. Be sure to vote for her."

"I will," Hannah said, smiling. The Blackberry Queen contest was relatively new, and Hannah wasn't familiar with it.

As her son started off, Elaine said, "Hold on a sec. Did you drop a blue UK hat in the barn?"

Blake halted, his brow furrowed. "No."

"What about Phoenix? Does it belong to him?"

Blake shook his head. "I don't think so. I've never seen him wearing a UK hat."

Mother and son were both starting to look agitated. "What's going on?" Hannah asked. It had to be about more than a ball cap.

Elaine tugged at the bottom of her blouse. "We're not sure. It's just that ever since Marshall wrote that article, strange things have been happening around here. Small, so you think you're imagining them, but definitely still happening. Right, Blake?"

He nodded. "Yeah. Like a door is open that I was pretty sure I shut. Things are moved around. Mostly in the barn but also the tool shed, tractor garage, and even Phoenix's cabin, according to him. Though he's a slob," he added. "So it's hard to tell if that's part of the weird stuff going on around here, or if it's just him."

Hannah was concerned. "Have you reported it to the police?"

"Reported what?" Elaine's shoulders rose. "Nothing's missing or even damaged."

"But someone was in your barn." The thought of an intruder was distressing. Whether they'd disturbed anything or not. Hannah couldn't think of a single good reason someone would want to sneak around another person's property.

"It was probably a customer. Or someone looking for one of the boys." Elaine pulled a couple of blackberries off a bush.

Hannah sensed Elaine was ready to close the subject. "Well, if things escalate…"

Elaine dropped the berries into a basket. "I know where you're going with that, and don't worry. My guard is certainly up."

Leaving it there, Hannah began to pick berries as well. Their baskets were almost full when Banjo let out a bark before tearing off across the field.

Elaine put a hand over her eyes to watch the dog and then groaned. "You've got to be kidding me."

Hannah turned to see what her friend was looking at.

A bareheaded man wearing sunglasses, a blue shirt with rolled-up sleeves, and loose canvas pants made his way toward them. When Banjo reached him, he stopped to greet and pat the dog.

"Who is that?" Hannah asked.

"My neighbor. Cooper Combs. Another thorn in my side. He recently moved back here from Louisville." Elaine continued plucking berries, her movements a little fiercer than strictly necessary.

"Should we run away?" Hannah joked.

That made Elaine smile and shake her head. "I wish. But it's better to get it over with. Otherwise, he'll hound me."

A motor sounded, and Hannah saw a small refrigerator truck back up to the barn door. The boys were loading produce as requested.

Cooper continued toward the patch. Once he reached them, he called out in a pleasant drawl, "Hey, Elaine. How y'all doing?"

Elaine raised her head. "Hi, Cooper. What's up? Oh, this is Hannah Prentiss. She owns the restaurant where I work. Hannah, this is my neighbor, Cooper Combs."

Hannah and Cooper greeted each other.

Cooper watched as Elaine returned to picking, hands in his pockets and rocking on his heels. Elaine wasn't making it easy for him, Hannah realized.

The longer he stood there, the redder Cooper's face grew. Finally, he burst out, "Elaine Wilby, you know as well as I do that your family stole those seeds from mine, and I want them back!"

A Note from the Editors

We hope you enjoyed another exciting volume in the Mysteries of Blackberry Valley series, published by Guideposts. For over seventy-five years, Guideposts, a nonprofit organization, has been driven by a vision of a world filled with hope. We aspire to be the voice of a trusted friend, a friend who makes you feel more hopeful and connected.

By making a purchase from Guideposts, you join our community in touching millions of lives, inspiring them to believe that all things are possible through faith, hope, and prayer. Your continued support allows us to provide uplifting resources to those in need. Whether through our communities, websites, apps, or publications, we inspire our audiences, bring them together, and comfort, uplift, entertain, and guide them. Visit us at guideposts.org to learn more.

We would love to hear from you. Write us at Guideposts, P.O. Box 5815, Harlan, Iowa 51593 or call us at (800) 932-2145. Did you love *The Key Question*? Leave a review for this product on guideposts. org/shop. Your feedback helps others in our community find relevant products.

Find inspiration, find faith, find Guideposts.
Shop our best sellers and favorites at
guideposts.org/shop
Or scan the QR code to go directly to our Shop

More Great Mysteries Are Waiting For Readers Like *You!*

Whistle Stop Café Mysteries

"Memories of a lifetime...I loved reading this story. Could not put the book down...." —ROSE H.

Mystery and WWII historical fiction fans will love these intriguing novels where two close friends piece together clues to solve mysteries past and present. Set in the real town of Dennison, Ohio, at a historic train depot where many soldiers once set off for war, these stories are filled with faithful, relatable characters you'll love spending time with.

Mysteries & Wonders of the Bible

"I so enjoyed this book....What a great insight into the life of the women who wove the veil for the Temple." —SHIRLEYN J.

Have you ever wondered what it might have been like to live back in Bible times to experience miraculous Bible events firsthand? Then you'll LOVE the fascinating **Mysteries & Wonders of the Bible** novels! Each Scripture-inspired story whisks you back to the ancient Holy Land, where you'll accompany ordinary men and women in their search for the hidden truths behind some of the most pivotal moments in the Bible. Each volume includes insights from a respected biblical scholar to help you ponder the significance of each story to your own life.

Mysteries of Cobble Hill Farm

"Wonderful series. Great story. Spellbinding. Could not put it down once I started reading." —BONNIE C.

Escape to the charming English countryside with **Mysteries of Cobble Hill Farm**, a heartwarming series of faith-filled mysteries. Harriet Bailey relocates to Yorkshire, England, to take over her late grandfather's veterinary practice, hoping it's the fresh start she needs. As she builds a new life, Harriet uncovers modern mysteries and long-buried secrets in the village and among the rolling hills and castle ruins. Each book is an inspiring puzzle where God's gentlest messengers—the animals in her care—help Harriet save the day.

Learn More & Shop These Exciting Mysteries, Biblical Stories, & Other Uplifting Fiction at **guideposts.org/fiction**